The New Kid

*To Jackie & Shawn,
Hope you enjoy my story.
Best Wishes!
Andrew Moss/Ben Anderson*

The New Kid

Reflections on an Eleven-year
Journey in a Children's Home

Andrew Moss

Copyright © 2014 by Andrew Moss.

Library of Congress Control Number:		2014909189
ISBN:	Hardcover	978-1-4990-2324-4
	Softcover	978-1-4990-2325-1
	eBook	978-1-4990-2322-0

All rights reserved. No part of this book may be reproduced or transmitted in any form or by any means, electronic or mechanical, including photocopying, recording, or by any information storage and retrieval system, without permission in writing from the copyright owner.

This book is based on a true story. However, names have been changed for the protection of all individuals mentioned in the narrative.

Any people depicted in stock imagery provided by Thinkstock are models, and such images are being used for illustrative purposes only.
Certain stock imagery © Thinkstock.

This book was printed in the United States of America.

Rev. date: 11/14/2014

To order additional copies of this book, contact:
Xlibris
1-888-795-4274
www.Xlibris.com
Orders@Xlibris.com
616620

This book is dedicated to all the adults who selflessly
served as houseparents at the
Burnside Children's Home.

PROLOGUE

Two ministers of a Conservative Evangelical Church established the Midwest Industrial Home for Children in 1876. The first residents were orphans from Chicago. After the turn of the century, the home began taking in more local residents. Eventually, the name was changed to the Burnside Children's Home.

Over the years, thousands of children passed through the home. Some stayed for only a few weeks, while some, like myself, stayed for many years. Majority of the children probably stayed for about six to eighteen months. Contrary to what most people thought, there were very few orphans at the home in recent years. Most children were products of broken homes due to divorce, adults having problems with the law, and economic problems or illness. It never occurred to me before, but I don't remember there being any children at the home, while I was there at least, who were physically handicapped. I find this surprising, but I guess it probably had to do with the fact that the home was not set up for handicap access unlike most homes today. There were many young people with emotional problems, some more severe than others. However, only a handful requiring more intense care for their problems had to be eventually transferred to other facilities.

Of all the other kids I lived with in my twelve years at the home, I only know where maybe a few dozen of them are today. People did not do a very good job of staying in touch with each other. A lot of the kids resented being there, and many were ashamed. One of the reasons for this short book is a hope that some of these people will become reacquainted. I also hope some of the kids who were resentful will take time to reflect and rethink their perceptions about the home. If there are young people out there who are in trouble or who have become separated from their families, I hope they will read my story and realize that life can get better. I hope my story will be an inspiration to them and to parents everywhere.

I walked into the bank, where I am a team leader of a group of commercial loan officers, on a typical day after Thanksgiving. The bank was quiet; no phones were going to ring today. Most of my customer's businesses were closed today. They weren't thinking about business, and really, I wasn't much in the mood either. I felt like staying home, eating leftovers, and watching movies. My wife, Alexis, had cooked a wonderful Thanksgiving dinner for me, her mother, and her brother's family.

My administrative assistant, Jackie, who is coincidentally my age, asked, "So how was your Thanksgiving?" I normally disdain people asking me about holidays, vacations, and personal time off. First of all, I tend to be a fairly private person. Secondly, I don't think people really care. They are just making small talk, of which I am not really a big fan at the office, but Jackie is a very genuine person and really did want to know. I told her.

"Dinner was delicious, and I enjoyed the day off with my wife. It just wasn't a very memorable day. Like most holidays for me, it was a lot of fuss and then a letdown."

She said, "It doesn't sound like an old-fashioned Thanksgiving—the kind we had growing up as kids, does it?"

I said, "Let me tell you about when I was a kid . . ."

HOW IT ALL BEGAN

It was a sunny day in the tiny village of Kingston, Illinois. Ms. Ravelin's big four-door, black-and-white Buick pulled up in front of the farmhouse. Our mom told us five kids she would be coming, but it really didn't register until three of us actually got in the car with the social worker and drove off. There was a lot of hugging and crying. We understood that we were being taken away from our parents. We did not understand the gravity of it all, but we all had known in our hearts that this was going to happen. We were all taken to Auburn, Illinois. I was taken to a foster home to stay with Bob and Doris Purtill. My sister, Linda, the youngest of the five kids, was taken to our maternal grandparents, Derek and Macy Bolden. Karen, the oldest, was taken to the Richard Still Children's Home in Auburn, Illinois. Michelle and Colleen remained at home for a short period. Michelle later went to live with our mom's only sister, Amelia, who lived in Auburn. Amelia and her husband, Dale, had three children of their own—Brett, Bill, and Jayne. Colleen joined me at the Purtill's a few months later.

The reasons we five kids were taken from our home were multiple. My dad was a chronic alcoholic. My mother, who would spend many years in a state hospital, had an IQ of only 69. Barely able to care for herself, she certainly was not able to raise five kids. She would never be able to function as a mother and would most likely never leave the mental institution. After high school, my mom entered a convent at some point. I think that would have been a good life for her. She was hardworking and kindhearted. She would have been taken care of and could have performed duties there that would have contributed to the convent's survival. I guess one evening she was out for a walk and met my dad. He was ten years her senior and apparently swept her off her feet. Marriage may not have been a bad option for her, if it was to the right man, but she and my dad were not good for each other. She certainly did not need to have five children, when she could barely take care of herself. My dad divorced my mom while she was in the institution. He, years later, gave up drinking and married a lovely woman and had several happy years of marriage. Out of nowhere, after seven years, he took to drinking once again. One subzero night in 1983, he got drunk, fell down outside of a bar, and froze to death. It is sad to say, but I somehow feel that he deserved that end.

There were a lot of bad times in our home; I really can't remember many, if any, good ones. My dad was drunk much of the time, and when he drank, he got mean. He and my mom argued a lot. My dad hit her on several occasions. Because of his drinking, there was never enough food, clothing, or basic necessities. My dad was always in trouble with his boss because of his drinking. Fortunately, we lived in a house on the farm that was provided as a job benefit. I recall a birthday of my mine when my dad took me to the grocery store with him. I asked for an inexpensive pair of gloves—the brown cotton with red lining. He didn't have enough cash, and the store owner wouldn't let him have any more credit. While I didn't fully comprehend the situation, I did feel the embarrassment. Even at that young age, that feeling bothered me more than not getting the gloves. My grandmother bought me a very nice red bike for my fifth birthday. I really liked it. It suddenly disappeared one day. I never knew for sure, but I think my dad probably sold the bike for drinking money. I remember another occasion when he took the coins from my piggy bank to go the bar. Our house was like the ones you see on the news where children are found home alone, in filth, with no food in the house. When I see those snippets on TV, I tell my wife, "That was our family situation."

Our family seldom went anywhere. We didn't go to church, unless we were visiting my grandmother. The only family friends were the occasional drunkards my dad would bring home, and that would generally turn into a brawl. I remember that on more than one occasion, my dad got into serious fights with people he brought home from the bar. My dad was always looking for a fight, even as a young man, according to his brothers and sisters. Fortunately, a couple of my aunts and uncles would sometimes drive up and take us kids back to their house in Milford, Illinois for weeks at a time. We all looked forward to these visits. I guess these same aunts and uncles would sometimes send my dad money to help out, and when they came to our house, they usually brought groceries. The visits continued for years, even after we were at the Children's Home. One place my dad did take me was to the tavern. By the way, the tavern is still there—the Blackberry Inn at the corner of Route 47 and Keslinger Road in Elburn, Illinois. I stopped there not long ago for a beer and a great hamburger after attending a Kane County Cougars game in Geneva, Illinois. Why he took me to the bar, I don't know. He thought it was cute to have me memorize dirty poems to repeat. I still have a propensity for telling jokes and remembering poems. I suppose my legacy from my father was the ability to tell jokes and a taste for beer. On the occasions that we would go to my grandmother's, my mom's mom, or to Aunt Amelia's, a fight would usually ensue between my dad and grandma or my dad and Uncle Dale. Holidays were never the happy times they were supposed to be. We kids liked going to visit our relatives. Their homes were always clean, there was enough to eat, and people got along. That is really all that we wanted in our lives.

I remember vividly one Sunday morning after my dad had been out drinking all night. He was driving the old red Farmall tractor around the barnyard, chasing the two work horses, one of whom was named Duke. He was going so fast that the tractor was leaning, and we were all sure it was going to tip over. Finally, the tractor ran out of gas. The horses eventually just returned to the barn as they would have anyway. At this point, Dad decided that he wanted chicken for dinner. He went to the barn, grabbed a hatchet from the workbench, grabbed a chicken by the neck, and laid it down on a tree stump located next to the front porch of the house. He then told me to hold the chicken still on the stump, which I did. Then splat! He had cut the chicken's head off. It was a bloody and violent scene for us kids. The expression, "Running around like a chicken with its head cut off" is true. Although the decapitation wasn't a very pleasant thing to see, seeing the chicken run around like that was somewhat amusing.

There is one incident in particular that I will always remember about my mom. Our mom was a very heavy-set woman with a big heart. Mom, Dad, and us five kids had been to a carnival or something. We had to walk home across the field from where the grade school was that we attended. I remember her gathering all five of us kids up into her lap and saying to us, "You kids will never end up in a home like some kids do." She must have had some idea at that point that we were going to be taken away because this was shortly before Ms. Ravelin came to take us away. To this day, my sister and I have a hearty laugh about this whenever we discuss it. It is one of the few tender moments I recall in my real home. I know that my mom was truly heartbroken when we kids were taken away.

It was inevitable that we kids would have to leave home. The conditions were deplorable. The house was never clean. I recall waking up at night to go to the bathroom and seeing rats running around the house. One time, a dead rat was found under my little sister's pillow. To this day, I have a phobia for rats and mice, dead or alive. Cockroaches were ubiquitous. Dirty dishes and laundry were always piled up all over the house. The television set seldom worked, and the phone was shut off a lot of the time. My dad always drove old cars that he constantly had to work on to keep running.

I'm sure there were two people who were primarily responsible for our being taken away from home, for which I am thankful to this day. The local grade school we attended apparently reported our plight to the authorities. We were sent to school unclean, our schoolwork unprepared, and of course, the town being very small, the teachers were well aware of my dad's drinking and my mom's deficiencies as a mother. The other person was Ms. Ravelin. She was not only the social worker for Kane County in Geneva, Illinois, but also her father was my dad's boss and landlord. I always thought she looked mean and didn't seem to care much for children, but I am sure that was just because of my age and her position. Between the two entities, I am sure they had no problem convincing the court that we would all be better off somewhere else than our own broken home.

Between the time that Karen, Linda, and I left home and the time that Michelle and Colleen left home, my parents apparently tried to live as a family unit. They were evicted from the farmhouse, and my dad was fired from his job. My dad drove them to Auburn; and for several days, my mom, dad and two sisters lived in the car and ate from a bushel of tomatoes that my father had stolen. During this period, as always, my dad had money to drink even though he neglected the basic needs of life of his family.

A NEW LIFE

On November 11, 1956, my oldest sister, Karen; my younger sister, Linda; and I were taken to the Burnside Children's Home in Burnside, Illinois. It was a gloomy, dark day. I don't recall being too scared. Even at that young age, I had a pretty positive outlook. Anywhere I had ever been besides home, I always found more enjoyable—school, the hospital, church, relatives, and the foster home. Why would I be unhappy here? We arrived in the middle of the afternoon. The other kids were still in school. We were each assigned a different housemother. Mine was Ms. Evans. Ms. Evans was young and very pretty. I was assigned a bed in a dorm of about fourteen beds. Each bed had a footlocker at the end for personal belongings, and I was assigned a drawer of my own in a communal dresser. A closet space was reserved for each person. The building was huge and seemed so lonely because no one else was there. Ms. Evans showed me around, took me to the kitchen, and gave me some cookies and milk. She introduced me to the cook and other adults. Everyone seemed very nice.

Shortly thereafter, kids started coming home from school. I found out immediately that my name had somehow changed. I was no longer Andy. Now I was the "new kid." That's how everyone referred to me for days: "He's the new kid." "Ask the new kid." "It's the new kid's fault." I soon discovered, however, that each time a new child came to the home, he or she automatically became the "new kid." That was the system. I no longer took it personally.

Most of the kids treated me okay. They knew I was in the same situation as they were. Some asked, "Why are you here?" They wondered if I had done something wrong or if my parents were divorcing or what my particular situation was. Most of the kids I met right away were young and hopeful. They had not yet developed the attitude that a lot of long-time residents came to accept—that they would always be in the home, and life was not going to get any better. These youngsters all felt that they would only be at the home for a short period. I wish that as adults we could maintain that optimism.

I soon learned about seating arrangements for the dinner table. Being the new kid did not earn you a guest status. Instead, you were forced to sit in what was referred to as "starvation corner." That is the last person to be served at the table. Unfortunately, by the time the food got to you, sometimes the bowl was empty. Most of the time, but not always, there was more in the kitchen, but you had to wait. Dinner time was quite formal. Table manners were observed. You cleaned up your own plate and took it to the dishwasher. Everyone stayed at the table until all children and the houseparents were done eating. Like in most families, discussions were about the day's activities in school. We talked about who got into trouble and things like that. Just like in a private home, the dinner table was a good place for the houseparents to learn more about what was going on in each child's life. The houseparent always sat at the head of the table and, of course, was served first. There was always a lot of nudging and kicking going on under the table—a silent way of communicating amongst the youngsters and letting others know that they should not talk about a certain subject or that they should not eat a certain item because one of the bigger kids had already claimed it. Sometimes, during prayer, fingerprints would magically appear on a piece of cake, marking that piece for one of the kids with more seniority. Food at the home was very institutional in nature. We had "square meals" daily. The fare was meat, potatoes, vegetable, salad, and dessert. The food was substantial enough, and we generally had enough to eat. That is, if you can ever fill up young and teenage boys. The food wasn't what I would call gourmet by any means. In fact, the kids from the Home were of the few who looked forward to the hot lunches at the high school. You could always tell the end of the month was coming or money was short because the food got worse. We would have more rice instead of potatoes, less meat, and on occasion, we had sauerkraut juice instead of orange juice once in a while. You haven't had a good start to your day if you haven't enjoyed a warm glass of sauerkraut juice for breakfast. On Sundays, we always had the main meal at noon, right after church services. This was always the best meal of the week because the management people of the home would join us. Most Sundays, we would have guests from the local church or visitors from another church.

Everything about the home was organized. There were about fifty kids at the home when I arrived—nursery through grade twelve. The groups were divided as follows: nursery, boys' first grade through fifth, girls' first grade through fifth, boys' junior high, and girls' junior high.

The nursery was closed shortly after I came to the home. I don't know the reason for this. All of these groups were in the main building. The teenagers were a block away in a building of their own. There were eight boys and eight girls, and their dorms were divided by a school-type fire door with an alarm attached. Each group had either a housemother or a married set of houseparents.

Meals, like most activities, were not only well planned but were also prepared, served, and cleaned up with the aid of, if not by, the residents. The girls helped in the kitchen to prepare dinner, served the food, set the tables, and cleared them. The older kids operated a large dishwasher. After I had this chore, I was allowed to run the similar dishwasher at the Old People's Home across the street. This was my first job at age thirteen. My pay was fifty cents an hour.

Chores were a very important aspect of life at the home. Each child had a daily chore. They included latrine duty, dishes, sweeping floors, garbage, kitchen help, and cleaning the yard. The list could go on. These chores had to be done before we were allowed to leave for school, do any kind of recreation or work anywhere outside the home. I feel this gave me a sense of responsibility that I never lost. Many of the kids resented these duties, but they never hurt anyone. As I got a little older, and smarter, I realized that if I got jobs away from the home, I not only had some spending money and freedom, but I could also get out of some of the mundane chore activities. Other kids resented those of us who had the initiative to find outside work, but that was their problem to deal with. I think the home was glad to have us working, supervised and be able to help with providing some of our own support.

The next day was a bright and sunny, but it turned out to be a cold day for I was taken to Kline Street Elementary School, a few blocks from the home. I was in the second grad, and my teacher's name was Mrs. Coons. The school was a large two-story building that had a new section and an older section. The new section held the gymnasium and recreation room. We walked to school and probably because of the school's close proximity to the home we also walked home for lunch. When I left the school for lunch, I apparently walked in the wrong direction and ended up by a factory, Burnside Die Cast, a couple of blocks away. I felt lost and was a little scared. Fortunately, the factory was letting out for lunch as well. A man dressed in a suit, shirt, and tie must have sensed that I was lost and asked if I needed help. I told him I was from the children's home and had lost my way. He pointed me in the right direction, and I turned around. Shortly, I caught up with some other kids who accompanied me home.

Living in a dorm was not the same as a college dorm. In college, you have two people to a room. Our dorms consisted of ten to fifteen beds. They were all close to one another, lined up on each side of the room. Depending on the population of the home at that time, the dorms could become very crowded. Each dorm had one bathroom for all inhabitants to use. One of the dorms had a bathtub, two sinks, and two toilets. The other dorm had just a toilet in a very tiny space no bigger than a closet. Both dorms had some built-in drawer space, and one had two closets with built-in cubby holes for each boy. There was a shower room located in the basement, two floors away. There was an old-fashioned, round water fountain where you could wash your hands, and there were four showers, as well as a couple of toilets. It was really kind of a spooky place to take a shower if you were alone. That part of the basement also housed lockers for our use and a ping-pong table. I became a very good ping-pong player because of the location of that table. We used it constantly. When I was in sixth grade, there was a ping-pong tournament at the junior high we attended. I made it all the way to the championship game, where I was defeated by an eighth grader. The other kids at school were pretty impressed by my skill. They were not aware that playing ping-pong was pretty much all I had to do. That's okay. I enjoyed the attention.

Living in a dormitory with ten to fifteen other boys, ages ranging from six to twelve, made for exciting nights. We had to start preparing for lights out half an hour before bedtime. We had to shower, put away our clothes and personal items, and quiet down. Then the houseparent would have some type of devotions. I think the devotions served two purposes. The religious aspect was part of the home's regimen, and the second purpose was to get us settled down and ready for sleep. When the lights went out, we were supposed to be absolutely quiet and go right to sleep. Right! Someone would let a loud fart, and that would start a chain reaction and turn into a contest of weird noises and awful scents. We had contests to see who let the loudest fart, the longest fart, or the smelliest fart. We were constantly short sheeting each other's beds, and we even learned how to set the beds so they would look normal but would collapse when a boy lay on it. This was even better when a houseparent occasionally sat on a bed that had been set. We had some great pillow fights. We would sneak out of our beds, crawl under other beds, and then scare other kids. When it was real quiet, you could even hear some of the boys masturbating, and there was on occasion some sexual experimenting that went on at night between boys. Sometimes we just talked and rehashed the day, or one of the boys would tell what happened at school that day, or we would quietly talk about houseparents or a new rule or procedure that had been made. A new rule was always a topic of discussion there. New rules really didn't change anything significantly, but it made for good conversation and something for us to complain about. As soon as one of the boys was aware of a new stricture, he would go around the home, saying, "New rule! New rule!" I guess we felt like that was our way of demonstrating. Sometimes you would hear someone crying during the night, probably lonely or thinking about his parents and wanting to go home. When we had a pillow fight or got too loud, it would wake up a houseparent, and then we were in trouble. The houseparent would ask, "Who started it?" Generally, there was silence. You learned at a very young age at the home that squealing was strictly forbidden by the other kids. Then we would get a group spanking. We had to line up one by one over the bathtub and get a spanking, usually one or two swats with a belt. Some of the boys cried; others did not. We became pretty used to the spankings. They didn't bother me in the group setting. We were all involved in the infraction, and the spankings were quick and didn't hurt that much. It bothered me more when boys were singled out for punishment for other things and then spanked. These spankings were usually longer and seemed more personal on the part of the houseparent. I thought the worst spanking episodes were the ones that happened after church services and before Sunday dinner. Mr. Klein used to do that when we were real young. He would single out kids from the dinner table who had acted up in church that day, take them to the basement, and spank them soundly. The kids always came back crying and then had to sit at the dinner table with the rest of us. They were not allowed to have dessert either. After he left the home, no one continued the practice.

THE POLICEMAN

Oh my god. That's him. What's he doing here? He's a cop?

To walk to Kline Street School, we kids had to cross an Illinois State Highway that runs through Burnside. There was always a policeman or two stationed at the crossing area to ensure our safety crossing the highway. On this particular morning, in the third grade, I looked up and noticed that I knew who the policeman was. He attended our church sometimes. The policeman looked right at me and said, "Hi, Andy." I almost wet my pants. How did he know who I was? Was he going to arrest me? Does he know of some mischief I had created? It had never occurred to me that a private person who attended our church on Sundays with his wife and family could also be a cop. His name was Tom Summers. He wasn't generally at the crossing, only occasionally after that. That didn't mean that I didn't see him anymore though. For the next forty years, Tom Summers was a constant in my life. He became my friend. I would see him at church, in school functions, and on patrol in his police car. Tom was always friendly, always called me "Andy" and seemed to genuinely like me. His wife, Mary, and his two children, Tom and Judy, both a few years older than me, were always friendly to me as well.

Several times while I was growing up at the home, Tom would drop off clothing for me that had been his son's. Tom would tell the houseparents, "These are for Andy." This made me feel special, especially since Tom and his son were very nice dressers. Those clothes made me feel like I was *in*. The irony of Tom and his son passing along clothes to me was that when I had my own men's store years later. Don became a very good customer of mine and looked to me for fashion advice. I felt honored to play that role in his life.

Like his dad, Tom became a policeman. Judy married and moved to Indiana. Mary, Tom's wife, worked at the county courthouse for many years but died at a fairly young age of natural causes. Unfortunately, Tom's life didn't turn out too well. He became involved with booze and drugs and eventually had to leave the force. He didn't pay his bills and became known as a deadbeat about town. This was unfortunate. An interesting side note to this story is that Tom and I looked quite a bit alike when we were in our twenties, and people would sometimes mistake me for him.

When I decided to enter politics, Tom was a supporter of mine. He couldn't officially support me since he worked for the City of Burnside, but several people told me that Tom Summers said they should "vote for Andy." Like his wife, Tom died fairly young too. I will always fondly remember the policeman and his family for their kindnesses and friendship.

THE COOTIE

"Don't touch him. He's a cootie!" ***What the hell was this about?*** I asked myself.

One of the older boys was yelling at another boy in a threatening manner. Mitch, the older and bigger boy, had taken it upon himself to determine who should be made a *cootie* and, therefore, punish him by not letting him associate with others. It didn't take me long to learn that there was an unofficial hierarchy existing even among elementary age kids at the home. The older boy, somewhat of a bully, would physically reprimand anyone associating with the deemed cootie. Thankfully, this situation was aborted by a houseparent after a time. In a setting like we had, with a lot of boys of varying age, size, and disposition, you were bound to have some bullies. I have to admit that I went through a stage of being a bully myself. There were a lot of boys with pent up anger and feelings of frustration, and they sometimes took this out on younger and weaker boys, sometimes girls. I guess this was a form of Darwinism in practice. I think that sometimes the bullying was a result of boys having been bullied or physically abused in their own homes. It was how they had been taught to deal with anger. Sometimes there were boys who were just plain bullies and probably always would be. For those of us who were just big for our age or who were going through a stage, we quickly learned that there is always someone out there who is bigger, stronger, or tougher and who will someday kick your ass.

During my fifth and sixth grade years, I grew very fast. I became strong and was big for my age. Growing up with older boys at the home had taught me how to fight and defend myself. I was used to doing physical labor, and my body was developing much quicker than most boys my age. I began fighting a lot. I also developed a very quick temper which got me into trouble at school. I was becoming a bully myself and was developing a bad reputation. I was punished both at school and at the home for my actions, but it kind of made me proud that I was bad or tough. Finally, one of my houseparents, Gerald Gates, a former marine and the brother-in-law of my best friend at the time, sat me down and had a serious talk with me. He explained to me that I was losing friends and the respect of my peers. He said if I continued fighting and getting into trouble, I would lose the privilege of playing sports. He also pointed out that if I continued fighting, I might seriously hurt someone and end up in jail for it. I had a lot of respect for Mr. Gates and took his advice to heart. I worked on my temper and quit being a bully. I did continue to defend myself through high school, and other kids respected my fighting ability. Today, people have a hard time believing that I went through this stage, as I have become pretty mild mannered and genial. Through the years, I have had the same conversation with other young people that Mr. Gates had with me. Hopefully, they took it to heart as I did.

SILVER DOLLAR

The store clerk asked, "What is that in your hand?" I could see he was looking at my 1921 Morgan silver dollar. The silver dollar I have been carrying in my pocket since 1959. I was in the fifth grade when Chester Gould, the author of **Dick Tracy**, who lived in Burnside, decided to give each child at the home a silver dollar for Christmas. Funny, I have never been that good at saving things, but somehow I have held onto this silver dollar for forty years! Years after I received the coin, Mr. and Mrs. Chester Gould used to shop in my men's store. I showed Chester the silver dollar. He was amused by the story.

He also drew me a little cartoon and signed it, which I kept on a bulletin board at the store. As I said, I was not a good saver, and I eventually lost track of the cartoon.

At one time, I had what I considered an extensive collection of baseball cards. I didn't own any real collector cards, but I had many, many cards and could quote a lot of statistics about some of my favorite players. I have no idea where the boxes of cards ended up. I probably traded them to one of the other boys for something I had become interested in at the time. We did a lot of trading and bartering amongst ourselves.

The one collection that I did hang on to was my stamp collection. I became a philatelist at the young age of nine. I collected stamps very seriously until I was about forty-five years old. When I sold my collection at that time, I had nearly 70,000 stamps in twenty-four albums. I got in trouble at the home on more than one occasion for ordering stamps without prior approval. I found that stamp collecting was a very educational experience and helped me at school in history, world events, and geography. While at the home, it gave me something I could call my own and enjoy by myself. Even as an adult, these same fields of knowledge were very useful, especially in games such as **Jeopardy!**, where answers to trivia questions were important. My ex-wife used to say, "If it is something you don't need to know, Andy knows it." I'm not sure that was meant as a compliment.

Kids at the home collected and saved all of the typical things that kids collect and save—stamps, coins, cards, rocks, dolls, bottles, matchbook covers, photos, records, and many other items. Most of the collections were just passing fancies as with most kids, but some, such as me with my stamp collection, became serious pastimes of children. One of the biggest challenges associated with collecting anything at the home was to keep it safe from other children. Some kids would steal items they thought might have value, some were just curious, and others just wanted to be mean and destructive. We all had some drawer space, a footlocker at the foot of our bed, and some closet space; but nothing was locked. With fifty kids, items had ways of disappearing. Sometimes kids would just destroy other kid's possessions out of jealousy and just plain meanness. As we got into high school, this became less of a problem because there were only two people in a room, and we could have locks and keys for our private or valuable possessions. Plus, with age, most of the kids became more aware and respectful of other's rights and personal space.

SCHOOL DAYS

The second and third grades were pretty unremarkable for me. Mrs. Freund was my second grade teacher, and we always got along well. Our paths crossed many times over the years as adults. Ms. Chickson, who walked with a cane, was my third-grade teacher. I passed the classes, made some friends, and started learning about life. For some reason, I can remember a lot about third grade. I recall the seating arrangements in the room and liking to read the Dr. Seuss books. I started growing faster and became more aware of other people and the differences in us. I did best in PE and found that I was a real good speller. It was a pretty typical educational experience for a youngster. My only real problem during elementary school was wetting my pants. This was a problem for years. During the fourth grade, the problem seemed to get worse. It got so bad that I would wet my pants while sitting in class, and the pee actually ran onto the floor. At one point, I was forced to wear a Kotex to try to contain the urine, and the other children referred to me as the "Kotex kid." This was very humiliating. My teacher, Ms. Dexter, took charge and demanded that something be done to correct the problem. I had some type of urinary surgery during the fourth grade and worked hard at the problem, and by the fifth grade, the problem was over. I didn't realize it at the time, but when I look back at my file from the home, the kids there found the urination problem to be irksome as well because of the odor. I tried to contain the odor by bathing several times a day. In addition to the physical problem, I am sure the bed and pants wetting was also a psychological problem caused by frustration and anger. It sure was a relief to be rid of the embarrassing situation.

It was in the fourth grade that I really started becoming aware of the world. Prior to that time, I was taken care of by someone else nearly all of the time. There really wasn't any thinking to be done. I didn't have to figure anything out for myself. Life was good, and that's all there was to it. By the fourth grade, I started having questions and wondering about things. I was noticing other people, getting interested in girls, seeing that life away from the home was different. In the fourth grade, we moved to the newer part of the school, and it just made you feel older, almost like you had moved on to junior high.

My fourth-grade teacher, Ms. Dexter, was a more serious teacher and had a more objective style than my former teachers who were more like baby teachers. Like Mrs. Freund, I had interaction with Mrs. Dexter as an adult as well. Additionally, I attended high school with her son and daughter, both very bright students.

The fourth grade was when I got a paper route. I delivered the **Burnside Daily Sentinel**, the local daily newspaper. I had a big route, delivering seventy-two papers each day. I collected .30 per week, and I got to keep .07, plus tips. I tried delivering the papers by bike, but I soon learned that I could provide much better service and, therefore, get better tips by walking the route. Some people wanted papers in their mailbox. Others wanted the paper between the doors. I soon learned a lot about customer service. I also won a couple of contests for selling the most new subscriptions and also for the least customer complaints. One of the prizes for winning a contest was supposed to be a trip to see a Chicago Black Hawks Hockey game. The event never happened. The circulation manager quit the day of the game. He not only quit but apparently absconded with the tickets and some cash from the company. I was learning how business really worked at a very young age. I also learned another job skill from being a paper boy that has always helped me in my career. I learned to do collections. People are no different about paying their paper boy than they are about paying anything else. I learned that I had to be persistent if I wanted to collect what I was owed. I found that I had to follow up on what people told me in order to get paid. Seventy-two papers was a lot, especially on Wednesdays when the grocery ads came out. One bundle of thirty-two papers went to Old People's Rest Home—the old people's home that was affiliated with the children's home. I had to carry the papers daily, but the residents apparently all paid ahead of time, so I didn't collect any tips. However, at Christmas time, I received an envelope with $32 inside. That was a large amount of money for a fourth-grade boy in 1958! I enjoyed my paper route. People were very nice to me. I got invited into their homes for pop and hot chocolate. Sometimes my route took a really long time on Friday nights when I did my collections because people would keep me at their homes for too long. Of course, there were a few grumpy customers, but for the most part, it was an enjoyable experience. For years, I had contact with a lot of my customers. Some became customers at my clothing store. A lot of them supported me when I ran for city council and mayor. Other adults got a kick out of it when some of these adults would call me Andy when they addressed me at city council meetings.

THE PREACHER

I walked up the porch steps to the house that was directly behind our little church at the Six Corners. Six Corners was the intersection of two highways and four local streets. There were six streets coming together, all with stop signs. No traffic light. This was a very unique traffic pattern, and every time a new reporter for the ***Daily Sentinel*** would come to town, he or she would have to write a story on the Six Corners. Years later, when I was serving on the Burnside City Council, I voted to close off two streets and install stoplights at the newly configured intersection. Naturally, this was progress and needed to be done, but I felt some sadness along with many other local residents. We were no longer ***Mayberry***. Our little town was growing up.

I rang the door bell, and surprise! The lady who answered the door was our preacher's wife, Mrs. Kingston. At the time, I didn't know what a parsonage was or why they lived there. She called me by name, said she was pleased that I was their new paper boy and that she was sure that Reverend Kingston would like to see me. She escorted me to the second floor office, going through the living room where their daughter Angel, who was several years older than me, was sitting on the couch. I always thought that Angel was very pretty, and I felt myself blushing. Reverend Kingston invited me in to his office. He was dressed in a suit and tie even while at home. He was working on his stamp collection. That was a nice surprise, as I had begun collecting stamps about a year earlier. Of course his collection looked very impressive and grand to me. He showed me his collection from Hungary that he was working on and even shared a few duplicate stamps with me. I visited for a while and then went on with my route. He told me I was welcome to stop by his home anytime, and I think he sincerely meant it.

I recall the first time I met Reverend Kingston. It was my first Sunday at the home. We had to walk about a block down to the church at the Six Corners. Reverend Kingston was the preacher. He was impressive with his nice suit, big voice, and likable personality. After the service, going through the greeting line, he pointed me out and said, "Who is this nice young man?" to my houseparent, Ms. Evans. He smiled, shook my hand, and told me that he came to the home quite often, and I could talk to him whenever I wanted. He spoke with sincerity, kindness, and authority. I knew I wanted him to be my friend. I saw him at church every Sunday. Most weeks I would see him visiting at the manor or going to the offices at the home. He always took time to speak to me. He would sometimes ask about my stamp collection. He always asked if I was being a good boy. He was a man who I wished could be my father.

Reverend Kingston and his family moved away from Burnside about the time I was in fifth or sixth grade. I missed seeing him. He was definitely a good role model, and I really looked up to him. While in junior high, he became the conference superintendent for our church and moved back to Burnside. He lived on Blainely Street, close to the high school and hospital. I sometimes visited him.

In another chapter of the book, I told about a pastor attempting to sodomize me. When I escaped that night, it was in Reverend Kingston's car that I spent the night hiding. The next morning, I went to his cottage and told what had happened the night before. Reverend Kingston, being the vigilant man that he was, immediately looked into the situation and found that there had been other reports about this pastor molesting young boys. The pastor was removed from the ministry, and the last I heard he was working as a librarian in a state university. After Reverend Kingston's tenure as conference superintendent was over, he took a pastorate at a church in Wisconsin. I only saw him sparingly for several years. He would occasionally visit the home and his daughter, Angel, who was married to a local young man. Coincidentally, she was married to the son of Tom Summers, the policeman friend of mine. People from the home and church would often tell me, "Reverend Kingston stopped by and asked, "How is Andy Moss doing?" It always made me feel good to know that he was still interested in my welfare.

In the early 1980s, Reverend Kingston retired and moved back to Burnside. He and his wife moved into his beloved Old People's Home for their golden years. He became a customer of mine in my clothing store, and I would see him often even though I was not attending the church any longer. He was supportive of me in my political career and was always curious about my four sisters and their welfare. Even years later, he would remember my sisters by name. Reverend Kingston was one of the bright spots in my life—a role model, mentor, and friend. Maybe one day we will meet in heaven and work on our stamp collections together.

THE RECORD

My final year at Kline Street School was interesting. It was during the fifth grade that I learned the home would not let us dance. The gym class had a section on square dancing. The kids from the home were required to sit and watch. We could not participate. I really did not know how to dance and didn't feel like I was missing a lot, but I did feel somewhat ostracized, and it made me feel different for the first time. It was the first time I felt ostracized as a result of being from the home. I didn't like that feeling. As I became older, the "No Dancing" became more of a problem. Because I was active in sports and had friends, I was invited to parties and dances. I, as well as other children from the home, was forbidden to attend these events. This caused dissonance between kids and houseparents. As I have grown older, I have seen what a silly rule that was, but the church ran the home, and that was their rule. I was learning the other meaning of the Golden Rule. They had the money; they made the rules. As I got into high school, I eventually was able to attend some private parties because parents of the host of the party would call the home and promise that I would not be allowed to dance. Of course I did dance. The other parents realized what a silly rule this was.

Darn, another spanking. All I did was slide down the back hallway bannister. How did she always show up at the times she did? Dizzy Dixon had caught me again. She was my fifth-grade teacher and also the school principal. Actually, her name was Marguerite. She was a nice lady and took an interest in me. Funny thing was she gave me thirty-three spankings in the fifth grade. I deserved them all and more. I was definitely "too big for my britches" at that time. I recall seeing Ms. Dixon downtown one day while I was in my twenties, and she said to me, "When I retired, you still held the record for spankings." She then winked. We always liked each other. She was a good teacher. I remember that she had wonderful handwriting. If you had Ms. Dixon for a teacher, you had good handwriting. To this day, people compliment me on my handwriting. She also sparked my interest in history and geography, which later became my strongest subjects. I recall studying all about the states in her class. I also remember that it was in the fifth grade that I kissed my first girl. Dale Washington and I were walking home from school. Cathy Rivers and Susie Stanger were walking in front of us. Karen was very cute and grew up to be a very pretty lady. We decided to just run up to them and kiss them. I kissed Karen, and Dan kissed Susie, and then we both ran off. We never found it if the girls liked it or disliked it.

PLAY BALL

I think one of the reasons I was able to overcome the wetting problem was because I was starting to develop physically and was growing up. I had joined Little League; I found that I was excelling at sports; I had taken on a paper route in the fourth grade, which I found stimulating; and I was already developing an interest in girls. My life was finally starting to experience some excitement instead of the dull and daily routine of life at the children's home. Joining Little League was one of the best experiences of my life. I found that I loved playing baseball and, fortunately, was pretty good at it. The first team I was on was the Tigers. We played at Stetson Park, a few blocks away from the home. I was able to ride my bike to the practices and games. Then I played for the Cardinals and Pirates. The Cardinals, in Division I, played at a local junior high field where I later attended. I was developing a few more skills by then. I played first base, probably because of my size. When I got to the Pirates, we got to play at Sullivan Field. Sullivan Field was in the city park and was relatively new. It had a home run fence—I hit a few over the fence that season—, a scoreboard, regular bleachers, a concession stand, and the field was lighted. It was almost like playing in the big leagues. I was lucky in that the teams I played on always did well, which always makes playing sports more fun. I made new friends and enjoyed my coaches—most of whom I would know for years to come. The coaches generally took an interest in me, and one of them started calling me Andy. The nickname stuck with me all through my sports career. I liked it. Being involved with Little League allowed me extra time away from the home and also afforded my some extra privileges, which I found very enjoyable. I played on the all-stars for two years and was allowed to travel out of town on the bus. I felt like I was playing major league baseball. During one of the seasons, the league took us to Comiskey Park to see a major league game. Wow, what an experience. It was many years before I got to do that again. I also discovered during

Little League that I could sell. We always sold candy bars as a fundraiser. In my second year of playing, I got my first new baseball glove because I won it for selling the most candy bars. I was always among the top sellers for years. Many years later, I coached Little League teams and served four years as president of the Burnside Little League. Coincidentally, I did a lot of fundraising for it at that point as well. Baseball was a part of my life for years. After Little League came Teener League for three years.

Teener League, I never liked that name, was great. We were the Tigers. Our manager, Jim Smith, had played minor league ball himself. He had four sons and was all about winning. He somehow was able to draft almost all of the top players from the previous year's little league team and get them all on the Tigers. We won the championship three years in a row. Jim taught us a lot about baseball along the way. I played first base all three years and did a little pitching. I was looking forward to moving on to Legion Ball.

Unfortunately, the year after Teener League, the local American Legion decided not to sponsor baseball any longer, so there was nowhere to continue playing hard ball in the area. I turned to softball. Until I was forty years old, I played softball every year in some venue or another. It was never as much fun as organized hard ball, but I enjoyed playing any kind of baseball. For some reason, as I grew older I became less of a hitter but a better fielder. I began playing third base instead of first base. I discovered that I had a very strong throwing arm and enjoyed playing third base. As much as I loved baseball, I was also becoming interested in football and basketball as well.

I entered the sixth grade at Stetson Junior High. However, I soon found that my love of sports became one of the only regrets I had growing up at the home. I didn't sense it as much as a kid as I do as an adult. As a youth, I was a pretty fair athlete. I found this a good way to become more accepted by my peers at school, plus the fact that I really enjoyed sports, especially baseball. The home didn't really encourage sports for two reasons. Because practices and games never coincided with the regimentation of institutional life, and because there was some organized play on Sundays, the home unofficially discouraged us from playing sports. Personally, I realized that the only way I could acquire any material things I wanted was by working. As a result of the home's discouragement and my desire to earn money, I gave up sports at age fifteen. This is a decision I have always regretted. I try to point out to young people that if they can make the choice, play sports. That enjoyable time of your life lasts only a few short years; you work for the next forty to fifty years. Perhaps because of this early decision in life, I have always put my work first. I will never regret, however, that I learned the importance and the necessity of hard work. I will never go hungry.

In the preceding paragraphs, I made references to the home forbidding us to dance and not allowing us to play organized sports on Sundays. The reasons for this were religious. The home was operated by the church, a fundamentalist religion that forbids alcohol, smoking, dancing, and most worldly sins. We were required to attend church every Sunday morning and evening. We were not allowed to attend movies until high school and then only if approved by Parents Magazine. Dating was officially very regulated. The home tried very hard to discourage boy-girl relationships, but with all those teenagers, a lot of relationships happened. Not all of the relationships that took place were boy-girl either. Many of us were exposed to many facts of life well ahead of most kids our age at the time.

THE BEST YEARS OF MY LIFE

In the sixth grade, I moved on to Stetson Junior High. Stetson, as we referred to it, was on the other side of town. It was well over a mile walk, but I didn't mind that. The sixth grade was an adjustment for me. I was big for my age. I was way beyond the maturity of a sixth grader. I had been exposed to a lot of adult parts of life already. I liked sports but couldn't participate on an organized level until I was in the seventh grade, so I turned to the wrong crowd. I started to hang around with the *greasers*. We didn't have gangs in Burnside, but these young people were the closest thing to it. They smoked, skipped school when they could, hung around with the *fast* girls, and got into more trouble with school officials and even the police than did most of the students. This was also the time when I was involved in a lot of fighting. Fortunately, this turned out to be a phase I was going through. It lasted through most of the sixth grade, and then I settled down and started playing sports seriously. It's funny when I think back as an adult about how sports affected my life. For a period of my life, sports provided me such joy and gave me the ego trip I needed so badly. Sports provided me with the two happiest years of my life. In eighth grade, I set two school sports records. One was for the Softball Throw and the other was in the 440-yard dash. I don't recall what the numbers were or how long the records lasted, but it was fun to have my name on the board in the gym. I knew I had a strong throwing arm, which came in handy for all the years I would play third base, but I had no idea I could run the 440. I just took off running and ended up setting the school record. Cool. In eighth grade, I was quarterback of the football team, and we were undefeated that year.

However, when I turned fifteen and I had to give it up so I could work and provide my own way, I simply turned my back on sports. I refused to attend high school sports events and games, I didn't watch sports on television for years, and I didn't hardly even discuss sports with my peers at work. Even today, I only pay enough attention to sports news so that I can carry on a halfway intelligent conversation with coworkers. The only exception is baseball. I still love that game and try to watch at least the all-star game, the playoffs, and world series.

I made a lot of friends in the sixth grade and found myself getting along better with the seventh and eighth graders because of my size and maturity. I liked the new junior high format of having different teachers and being able to move about the school rather than being in one classroom all day. We were able to have pick-up basketball games at noon, and there were a lot more girls to get to know. I didn't do well scholastically. I actually flunked English in sixth grade. I just didn't like it. It is funny because as an adult, I find that I have much better English, writing and punctuation skills than most of my coworkers. In seventh grade, I flunked typing. This is amusing because I have always been a good typist. I flunked because I didn't do the homework. Typing homework was difficult at the home because we only had one typewriter to be used by all the different kids, several of them taking typing at the same time. I liked my English teacher, Mrs. Wolf, but had no interest in the subject. During the sixth grade, I went through a stage of being the class clown. I felt it was my duty to entertain the whole class by speaking out of turn and making smart remarks. I paid for this with my bad grades. I wished I had realized then what a mistake that was. I spent the next two years in the slower sections of the seventh and eighth grades. If I had been put into the faster sections, I might have learned to be a better student.

I loved seventh and eighth grades. I really liked junior high. I was a teenager. I was in junior high. I was big for my age. I was good at sports. I made friends easily. I liked the girls, and they seemed to like me. I was working odd jobs and always had some money in my pocket. Life was the best it had ever been for me.

While life at junior high was so good, it was becoming a more difficult time at the home. My interests and accomplishments were not necessarily coinciding with the rules and regulations of the home. I wasn't doing anything wrong. It was just that I was all of a sudden operating on a different schedule and doing things that other kids had not done. This just created a unique situation. **Unique** does not fit in well in an institutional setting. Because of after school sports practices and games, I was not home at dinner time. That meant that food had to be saved for me. That was a big deal. I had extra laundry, and the uniforms had to be clean for games. That didn't fit the laundry schedule. Some of my sports events were scheduled for Sundays, which was a definite problem. Looking back, I guess the home had a real dilemma concerning my playing sports on Sunday. They wanted to follow the rules of the church, but they did not want to ostracize people at school or in the community either. Additionally, other children became jealous because they thought I was receiving special attention and special privileges. This situation was a problem all through junior high, but we all survived.

    I played football and basketball, playing first string on both for two years. In the spring, I played in the Teener League Baseball. When time allowed and I wasn't doing odd jobs, I would play sports with friends at their homes or at public parks or playgrounds. I played all the intramural sports I could at school and played in any church-related sports events. Sports were a huge part of my life. I enjoyed them, and they really helped me fit in at school and become popular. It was good for my ego. There were a couple of other boys at the home who were good in sports too. For one year, during the seventh grade, Steve, Cliff, and I made quite a splash at school. I remember we even had our names mentioned at church on Sunday after we had all had a very good football victory. We all played first string on the football, basketball, and baseball teams and dominated the intramural sports program. We were popular with other guys, girls, and teachers. We did a lot to bring some good PR to the home. Steve, Cliff, and I spent a lot of time together. We were proud of ourselves and worked hard. Unfortunately, Steve's family left the home and went back to Chicago. Cliff, who didn't live at the home, but his parents worked at the Old People's Home, moved back to Kansas with his family. Cliff was my best friend. I really missed him. He went on to have a fine sports career in college. I don't know what happened to him after that. Steve didn't fare so well. He eventually ended up in prison for car theft. If Steve and Cliff hadn't moved away, perhaps I would have stuck it out with sports.

    In addition to sports, my music was going well while in junior high. Because of singing in church, my voice had a chance to develop. My voice changed earlier than most, and I began taking voice lessons while in seventh grade. I took them from a local man who taught music at Hester High School, a few miles north of Burnside. I could not understand why a man with this kind of obvious talent was teaching at Hester, in a town of 600 people. I eventually found out. He had had an affair with a student at another school previously. This student was now his wife, Linda. Anyway, Mr. Schuman was talented and spent a lot of time with me. I could have done better as a student. While I liked what I was learning, music and sports were not always cohesive in nature. Yelling was not good for my voice. Sometimes we had choir practices or programs that conflicted with sports scheduling. I always seemed to go with the sports. Moreover, practicing my voice exercises didn't go over well with other kids at the home. It was very intrusive for me to be doing them at any time, so I just didn't practice as much as I should have. At school, I sang in the choir, a male quartet, and for school functions. When I look back to that time of my life, it probably would have made more sense to put more effort into music, as one can sing and play the piano well into older age. However, the physical attributes needed to play sports fade away quickly. I feel badly that I did not respond fully and give back the devotion to some of the adults that they deserved for giving me special attention and trying to make my life better. I wish I could have a couple of those opportunities back again, but I also realize that many kids must go through these same processes, certainly at home, if not with other people. It is just part of the growing-up process.

Junior high at Stetson was the best three-year period of my life. Everything seemed to go my way. I thought life was great. Despite the fact that I was living in a children's home, I was learning that I could still be popular, successful, and enjoy life.

THE HARD YEARS

After my wonderful seventh and eighth grade years, my freshman year at Burnside High School was quite an adjustment. I had moved to the Heston House for teenagers, I was working a couple of part-time jobs, I had a steady girlfriend, and I was becoming very curious about life. I also was no longer the "big man on campus." There were a lot more students in high school. Bigger guys and better athletes were everywhere. There were more teachers and administrators. Everyone didn't know me like in junior high. It was going to be a lot harder to prove myself. The courses were tougher. There was a lot more to choose from in the courses. There was more homework. I really was not ready for high school. I had too much fun in junior high and did not prepare well. Sadly, my four years in high school were not memorable. I always had a circle of friends, and I had some success with my musical career, but by and large, I could not wait to get out of high school. At this point in my life, I really could have used a father or a set of parents. I wasn't getting good direction on a regular basis. We had counselors at school who would speak with you when you were in trouble, which happened more than it should have in my case, and we had social workers at the home we could talk to, but it was difficult to have one-on-one time with them because they had fifty children to counsel. Plus, the fact that all the kids were apprehensive about opening up too much with the home's social workers because we were afraid they might pass on information that would get someone into trouble.

My high school years were challenging for me in a lot of ways. I went through the typical kinds of conflicts every high school student goes through, but at the time, it seemed like I was the only one having these conflicts. I'm sure every high school student feels the same way. There were such big quandaries. Do I go to college? Should I drop out and just get a job? Do the girls like me? Should I ask Nancy out? What if she says no? What does the home and the church see wrong with dancing? Why doesn't someone adopt me? Why do the teachers load us up with so much homework? I thought high school was supposed to be fun. I found it boring, too much work and full of emotional pressures.

Wading through the rough waters of high school caused me to make a lot of bad decisions and make a few mistakes. I gave up sports, I didn't take the right courses, I didn't choose the right friends, I sometimes acted like a clown in class, and I got into fights. I was fortunate that I could get by with my grades without really even doing much homework. This did not turn out to be a good strategy, as I learned when I went off to college that I was not well prepared academically. For many years, I never blamed the home, and I refused to be angry at anyone. I just figured that this was my fight to get through life, and I had to deal with it as best as I could. Years later, I am beginning to see that I made some less than smart decisions earlier in my life that I probably would have done differently had I had a real set of parents to help guide me. At age sixty-five, I am just now beginning to harbor resentment about that situation.

I liked going to school each day in order to get away from the home, the same kids, and the same routines. I had friends at school that I liked to associate with, but my mind was always elsewhere than school. I was always thinking about girls, my part-time jobs, more about girls or other activities. I never had problems finding dates in high school, but the process wasn't that easy since we were limited in our activities, and transportation was always a challenge. As a result, I found it convenient to be involved with girls at the home, even though the home took a dim view of the situation. When my friends became old enough to date, double dating in their cars helped. I occasionally was able to borrow someone's car. That was really nice. When I bought my Honda motorcycle in my junior year, the girls liked riding on it, but it was not really conducive to dating. Because of all my part-time jobs, I always had money for dating, which helped. Having money always impressed my friends too. It's really ironic that I was the kid from the children's home, but I always had money in my pocket. Actually, I wasn't supposed to have cash. It was all supposed to be turned in to the houseparents immediately. I guess that the **underground economy** was at work even when I was in high school. Sometimes I think some of my friends just liked me because I furnished cigarettes and bought cokes after school.

"Mary, how are you? I haven't seen you in years." I was happy to see Mary, one of my classmates from high school. We were never close but always friendly. Mary was very nice and always on the honor roll all through school. Mary said to me, "My mom told me that you are now the mayor." I told her that was correct. She said,

"You know, Andy, when we were in high school, no one ever figured you would be mayor one day." I laughed, but the comment actually hurt my feelings. The hurt was my own fault, and I deserved it. However, her comment kind of summed up my high school years, pretty much of a disappointment for me and everyone around me. I sometimes wish I could go back and have the chance to do better. Again, I wasn't getting the right direction; and when I was getting help, I didn't have sense enough to take it. Even though high school was, in general, a hard time for me, there were a few bright spots.

I have often told people that I would go back to high school today if I could go through Coach Bosker's gym class again. This class provided more entertainment and laughs than one can imagine. It was kind of like *Porky's* the movie, only in real life. Coach Bosker was the athletic director at the high school. He was near retirement age at this time but had had a distinguished career as an athlete and coach in his younger days. He originally was at Dodd School for Boys, which had been a private school for boys, located in Burnside for many years. The school closed in the early 1950s, and Coach Bosker transferred to Burnside High School. The Dodd School property was adjacent to the children's home property, and the children's home actually took over some of the property. The Anderson House, where the teenagers lived, was purchased from Dodd School. Dodd School was quite famous in its heyday. One of the more famous residents was Orson Wells, the actor. At one time, I had a set of Orson Wells's report cards that I had found stuffed away in an old safe I was required to clean out. I remember that his grades were average, and the teacher made the comment that he "had a dirty mouth." A former employer of mine remembered Orson Wells as a child. He said he was quite eccentric for a young person. He remembered Wells wearing a rope for a belt and said he always seemed to be daydreaming whenever he was seen about town.

By 1963, Coach Bosker had become quite bent over with age, had lost some hearing, and was really ready for retirement. I think he was smarter than he let on with us though. I think he put up with our shenanigans just because he liked young men growing up and enjoying themselves. The six-week course on swimming was an absolute riot. There was hardly a day in that whole period that I was not kicked out of the class for the day, and most days, one or more of my friends were invited to join me. On the first day of class, Coach told us that the boys who didn't know how to swim should gather at the shallow end of the pool. I said to one of my friends, "Hey, let's have some fun." We went to the shallow end of the pool and immediately started dunking the heads of the boys who couldn't swim. Day one, Kenny and I were sent to the showers early. One day, we used the benches that were for swim meet viewers as canoes. That didn't go over well either. Coach would sit his chair on the end of the diving board during class. He would have us line up, three on each side of the diving board, and he would say, "Okay, on three, dive." "One," and one of us would dive. He would chastise that one. "Two," and someone else would dive. This scenario would last most of the class, allowing very little actual instruction to happen. The other boys in the class always enjoyed this spectacle. Another time, we unlocked the windows, which were painted over and locked, that adjoined the school cafeteria. This was especially amusing since we were required to swim in the nude. That incident delighted a lot of high school girls and got me and another guy sent to the principal's office for detention. The punishment was worth it. During the track portion of gym class, we would sneak under the bleachers and smoke cigarettes. One time, Coach walked by and asked what was going on. We said, "It's cold. You can even see your breath out here." I'm not sure he fell for the smoke being our breath, but he just sent us on. I could go on and on about Coach Bosker's class and the fun we had there, but there are other stories to tell.

Ms. Flyer was a biology teacher. She did not have the advanced students. We had biology in our sophomore year, so by that time, we had heard that she did not have much control over her class, and it was easy to cut up. My friend, Randy, and I were ready for the class on the first day. When the sign-up sheet was passed around, I wrote the name Fonda Peters on the list. Ms. Flyer kept asking, "Is Fonda Peters here today? Is anyone Fonda Peters?" The students had a good laugh, but Ms. Flyer just shook her head and said, "I guess Ms. Peters is not here today" and moved on. Another time, I asked Ms. Flyer, while studying anatomy, "What are those bumps on the lady mannequin's chest?" She went on to explain about mammary glands to us, and she made it even more comical because she kept touching the bust. Again, this created quite a humorous class event. Finally, after several weeks, Ms. Flyer kicked me out of her class. I was in the principal's office the next day during her class period, and she came in. She said, "Andy, I have the nicest young man who will be your new lab partner."

I said, "That's nice. What's his name?"

Ms. Flyer said, "His name is Wayne Rice." I almost fell off my chair. Wayne and I were the primary instigators of trouble in Coach Bosker's class. Again, I could go on and on with stories about Ms. Flyer's class, but suffice it to say that her world did not improve after Wayne and I became lab partners. Somehow, I passed biology, but I have to admit that I am a bit ashamed of myself for taking advantage of her the way I did.

"Bang!" The firecracker went off, scaring Eddie Duncan nearly to death. It woke up the kids who usually slept through 314 study hall. You really had to know Mr. Duncan to appreciate this story. He was a social studies teacher—very quiet and reserved, timid really. He was in charge of the study hall, located in room 314, which housed about one hundred students. Mr. Duncan hated fresh air and any kind of noise. We used to roll pennies down the aisles which would give him the creeps. Then two or three of us would drop our books at the same time. This would about give him a heart attack, but the firecracker incident was the best. I had gotten up to sharpen my pencil. I then opened the window. Mr. Duncan, in his very unique squeaky and strained voice, said, "Mr. Moss, please close the window." Not only was his voice amusing, but he had this habit of shaking a crooked finger at the air when he talked. He could have been a cartoon character. I closed the window as instructed. Then my friend, Randy—yes, the same one from biology class—sharpened his pencil and opened the window. Again, Mr. Duncan asked that the window be closed, all the while shaking the crooked finger in the air. The other students were beginning to sense something was going to happen. This heightened the drama. Finally, I got up again to sharpen my pencil. I could feel Mr. Duncan's eyes watching me. I sharpened the pencil, glanced to Randy for the signal, then opened the window, and set the firecracker under it. This time, Mr. Duncan jumped from his chair while I returned to my seat. He grabbed the bottom of the window and yelled, "I want this window closed," and proceeded to slam it onto the firecracker. The noise really wasn't that loud, but the effect was thunderous. That incident got Randy and I expelled from school for a couple of days. Again, it was worth it.

I wasn't the one to pull this next stunt, but Mr. Duncan was pretty sure that I was involved, though I was not. During social studies, Mr. Duncan used the pull-down maps that were always in school classrooms at the time. One day, before class started, one boy brought in a nude photo of a woman that was taken out of a Playboy Magazine. He strategically placed it over the map of the country we were studying that day. Several of us knew of the prank ahead of time and were telling our classmates to pay special attention when we got to the map portion of the class. Well, it worked as planned. Mr. Duncan got up from his desk about halfway through the class, went to the maps, and said, "Today, we are going to talk about East Germany," and pulled down the map. He took one look and nearly fainted. Truthfully, I am not sure that he had ever seen a naked lady before this. He let go, and the map snapped back into place. He took his seat, and not another word was said for the rest of the class. I wonder if he took the picture home with him that night.

I was expelled from high school another time. One of my friends, whose parents went to our church and whose father was on the school board, blew white powdery frosting from his brownie on me. I don't know why I reacted the way I did, but I got up and punched him right in the face. Bryce and I had been friends since the second grade. His parents and older brother had always been nice to me. I just overreacted. It was more of that pent-up anger and frustration I guess. Needless to say, you don't punch out the president of the school board's son without getting expelled. I apologized to Lynn two days later, and we continued to be friends. In fact, whenever Bryce would come back to visit his parents, he always looked me up. I feel bad about the day that I hit him.

MULTIPLE PERSONALITIES

With the diverse backgrounds of the many children, there was a multitude of personalities and temperaments. There were many clashes of wills and personality conflicts. Some of these naturally turned into fistfights, and the physical fights were not always between boys. We had some pretty tough girls that came through the home, and I think some of these had plenty of experience fighting off boys and men who had made unsavory advances in the past. While the home did not condone this, there was certainly enough fighting that one learned to take care of oneself. We did have a couple of sets of house parents who let us put on boxing gloves and fight it out. It really was a good way to release a lot of pent-up frustrations. Most of the boys fought it out, and that was the end of it. The girls, however, were a different story. Their fights were generally more vocal and lasted longer. They were more spiteful and held grudges. With the boys, the fight was history the next day. When the girls fought, they would be referring to each other as **slut** or **whore** for a week. They would try to turn other girls against their opponent by gossiping or lying about them. I express the same observation about disagreements with houseparents. The boy's fights with houseparents were short, but the girls were more serious. They always wanted to hurt each other, would hold grudges, and would attempt to turn others against the one there was a problem with. In this regard, It sure seemed to me that raising boys was much easier than raising girls.

These diverse backgrounds also caused more behavior problems. We had kleptomaniacs, a nymphomaniac, and a pyromaniac among us. Those I know for sure. How many other **maniacs** we had, I am not sure. However we did have an occasional squad car at the home, usually for shoplifting. Runaways were very common. Most never even made it out of town and were returned within twenty-four hours. I'm not sure why, but I never even entertained the idea of running away. My sister, Colleen, ran away once but, like the others, was returned promptly.

More girls ran away than boys. Again, I think this had to do with the differences in the emotions of the two sexes. When the girls were angry, they wanted change or revenge right away, whereas the boys seemed to accept situations more easily. I would say that 75 percent of the girls who lived at the home ran away at least once, but several ran away multiple times. One girl told me recently that she and another girl just ran away because they "were bored that day." When boys ran away, they usually went alone and were generally more successful. The girls almost always ran away in couples. I suppose they were easier to spot by adults and police traveling together is the reason they were generally returned within twenty-four hours.

One time, two girls, Tina and Melinda, ran away to Chicago. They wanted to look up a family of kids who had recently left the home, the Wagners. The Wagners lived in Chicago. I don't think the girls even had an address. I guess they just thought they would find the other kids standing on a street corner. The cops found the girls on a street corner in the loop. Unfortunately for the girls, they were taken to a home in a neighboring county. The Audy Home was not like the Burnside Children's Home. The girls were strip searched, and they had a vaginal exam done. They were made to wear uniforms and were just left to sit in their rooms, more like cells actually, for forty-eight hours. Finally, one of the girls called the executive director of the home and begged to come back, promising that she would never run away again. She never did run away again after that.

Tina was a very pretty girl who made friends easily. She hung around with a group of girls at school on a regular basis. In a conversation with her recently, she told me that one of the girls was actually hidden out in the girl's dorm for a week. The people at the home didn't know it and neither did the girl's parents. Tina said that this girl told her that she wished she could live at the children's home rather than her real home, where life was so bad. Tina also told me of another girl who was adopted by one of the home employees had expressed to Tina that she always wished that she lived at the home rather than where she did. Stories like these are real testaments to the good way that the home treated and took care of us.

Really, for as many children as went through the home throughout the years, there were very few problems in the community. I guess that is why the community was supportive of the home.

When I think about the difference in the way the girls and the boys reacted to adverse situations, my thinking is fortified by conversations I have had with some of my former alumni regarding their stay at the home. Again, the men just seemed to accept it as a part of their life. Some of the women, however, still feel they were a victim and hold an angry grudge against society.

    I had a multitude of houseparents over the years. I had a single woman, college students, and married couples. Some were part-time, some full time. Having so many sets of parents made it difficult to form lasting relationships. I think, as a result, I learned to emotionally turn my feelings off rather than become attached and be hurt. Many times at school, I felt I was fortunate I was raised where I was because I didn't have the heartbreak and emotional ups and downs experienced by some of the other kids. If I had a difference with a houseparent, it would usually blow over, and that would be the end of it. If I didn't especially care for a particular houseparent, I would just avoid any more contact than was necessary. No emotional scars. I recall very vividly hearing friends at school talking about fights and disagreements they had had with their parents. I always felt bad for them and was glad that I didn't have to go through that. Then again, at the same time, I couldn't help but wonder if I had a real home of my own if I would have the same problems or if somehow it would be better. I would like to have known.

FIRE

"Fire! Fire!" Someone was yelling on the playground from around the other side of the main building. You could hear him clearly, but he was probably one hundred feet away and around the corner of the massive building. I ran around to where he was, and Wow! Annie Kugler's house was ablaze. No fire trucks were there yet, and the haunted house was really burning fast. The volunteer fire department finally did show up and put out the fire, but the house was destroyed. We all knew who did it because he said he was going to do it one day. His name was Doug, and he had a fascination with fire. He liked to use a magnifying glass to burn leaves. I believe we have all done that. He was always getting a hold of a book of matches, which, of course, were not permitted, and trying to set something on fire. There are two interesting side notes to this story. The first being that the last thing I ever heard about him was that he was in prison for arson; he had burned down a vacant commercial building in the town where he lived. After the fire, Annie Kugler reestablished her residence in the attic of the decades-old main building. We were always more than willing to share this information, especially late at night with all new kids.

MONEY, MONEY, MONEY

The home was always short of money. They did many things to raise funds. The two main areas of support came from the church and the counties who sent children to the home. Another fundraiser was tagging. In the fall of each year, the home would send teams of us to other communities to collect money by standing on street corners with a can asking pedestrians, "Would you like to contribute to the Burnside Children's Home?" Several of us would be taken in a car to a neighboring town, where each of us would stand at a busy corner. The cans had a slit in the top through which people could drop coins, or occasionally, a dollar bill. I believe we are all familiar with the phrase, "God helps those who help themselves." We sometimes used these tag days to help ourselves. We felt we were eliminating the middleman, so to speak. We did this by slipping one of the tags into the slit of the can and tipping it upside down. This would usually yield a handful of coins. The other trick was, on the rare occasion that someone offered a bill instead of coin, we simply offered, "Oh, let me do that for you." I doubt that we ever fooled anyone. Maybe they had heard the old adage too. Most of the kids really hated tagging. I actually kind of enjoyed it. It was a way to get away from the boredom at the home. I got to see different communities and sometimes met new people. Over the years, I have been a very successful fund-raiser for a lot of organizations, and I think part of the reason is that at an early age I learned to ask people for donations. Most people absolutely hate to ask others for money. The tagging stopped for some reason while I was in high school. I don't know the reason for sure, but I would suspect that the State of Illinois probably had misgivings about sending children out in strange communities like that.

Always being in a pinch for money, the vehicles the home had were always old and in need of repair. At some point, someone donated a bus.

I'm sure they accomplished two things—one, being a tax deduction for the donor; and second, being a place to get rid of the clunker. The bus was used for everything—trips to the lake, rides to school when it was zero degrees or colder, rides to church camp, occasional field trips, and whatever function there was for us to attend as a group. It was great that all the kids could go in one vehicle. What was not great was that the bus broke down nearly every trip. Naturally, everyone who rode the bus, kids and houseparents alike, viewed these trips with great apprehension.

Holidays and special occasions were usually not very special at the home. There were simply too many kids, but the home always remembered our birthdays. They would see that we got a present and had a cake. Even though the home was always short of money, they always made attempts to make birthdays and holidays special for us. As I have grown older, I have learned that many times we were remembered better than a lot of kids in private homes. Each June, there were graduation parties, as there was always someone graduating from either junior high or high school. Fourth of July, Memorial Day, Labor Day came and went. Don't get me wrong. We were not neglected. We got tickets to circuses, carnivals, ball games, fireworks, or whatever event came to town. However, most holidays when families get together, were just another day for us. Christmas was different. Each year prior to Christmas, each child was asked to submit a wish list. These lists were then distributed to churches, local clubs, and organizations such as the Moose, Kiwanis, and Elks, as well as private individuals in the community and church members. Usually, on the eve of the last day of school before Christmas, the home would have a Christmas party. Entertainment would be provided, Santa Claus would visit, a really nice dinner was prepared, and each child received a huge bag of gifts, toys, clothes, games—you name it. While we didn't receive large gifts such as stereos, TVs, etc., we were given very nice gifts. In addition, many organizations gave us parties and more gifts. The home and all of these organizations and individuals certainly did their part to make some wonderful memories of Christmas as a child. The Moose, Elks, Kiwanis, VFW, the Grange, and other local groups had wonderful Christmas parties for us. We would have a very nice dinner, a Christmas program, and would all go home with presents. We had very nice Christmases in my mind. Being the age that I am now, I know for a fact that there are many, many children and adults who will never have as good a Christmas as we kids enjoyed at the home.

I recently spoke with one of the kids who was a child of the executive director's secretary. Deanna's dad, who was a large man and a very kind and good-natured fellow, always played Santa Claus at our annual Christmas party. Deanna told me that she resented the fact that her dad was never home for Christmas Eve because he was always at the home playing Santa Claus. She also remembered one Christmas that she wanted a particular child's oven. She didn't get one, but one of the girls from the home did. Deanna was very upset about this. She also told me that she wished as a child that she could live at the home because the kids always had things to do. She felt like an outsider. I found her outlook very interesting since all of us kids wanted to live in a home like hers. As the saying goes, "The grass is always greener on the other side of the fence."

NEAR-DEATH EXPERIENCE

There was a family of four boys at the home. Darrell, Les, and a set of twins named Bob and Bo. They had an uncle from Chicago who used to visit on a lot of weekends. He was a prince of a guy. He always brought things for his four nephews and also for other kids. I remember one time he brought out about a dozen transistor radios and passed them out to several kids. One weekend, the roommate of the oldest brother was gone for the weekend, so their uncle decided to spend Saturday night in the bottom bunk of the bunk bed. Everyone had gone to bed. It was about 11:00 p.m. The roommate unexpectedly came home. The roommate was a bit of a bully and wasn't always even tempered. He came into the room with just a lamp on for light. He saw someone in his bed. Thinking it was one of the other kids who had decided it was okay to sleep in his bed since he was away, he grabbed the occupant of his bed by the throat and proceeded to give him the scare of his life. Larry told me later that he could see the guy's eyes bulging but didn't realize yet who it was. Finally, the nephew woke up and calmed down his roommate. Maybe it's my imagination, but it seemed like the uncle's visits became less frequent after his brush with death.

COVERT DATE

The home was apprehensive about dating. They also didn't like us doing much on Sundays. They certainly didn't want us dating on Sunday. My roommate, Chance, both of us about age fifteen, and I, had girlfriends who were friends. One of their parents was away for the weekend, so we decided to meet at her house that afternoon. As we were leaving church, we made arrangements to stop out and see a couple of guys from one of the better church families. It just so happened they lived close to my girlfriend. Our houseparent actually gave us a ride out to our friends, so we had great cover. We did visit our friends for a few minutes and then moved on to our real destination. After a great afternoon, we made it home on time, feeling smug in the realization that we had attained our goals for the day and no one was wiser. That night, after church our friend's mother walked up to our houseparent and said, "It was nice of the boys to stop out this afternoon, but they sure didn't stay long." Our houseparent, knowing we were gone for nearly four hours, immediately grounded us both. I often wonder if the parent of our friends didn't purposely get us in trouble. That was probably the case because her husband, who owned a tile business downtown, was always tattling to houseparents about the actions of kids whom he would observe. There was another scary aspect to the story. My girlfriend's parents owned a funeral home. They lived upstairs. Unexpectedly, the parents came home early that day. Chance and I had to take a detour through the basement where there was a dead body. We sure had fun with the girls but the rest of the day didn't turn out too well.

DONATIONS

The truck had arrived with the clothing that came from Whiston College. We always knew when it was coming and watched for it. Upon its arrival, someone would always yell, "Donations." Everyone knew to run to the laundry house and get in line. Usually, a houseparent would divvy out the items as he or she felt appropriate. On a Saturday morning, once a month, the truck would arrive from Whiston College. It was full of clothes that the students would donate to the home. We would occasionally also get a donation from the Salvation Army. Once in a while, a church or community organization somewhere would do a clothing drive for the benefit of the kids at the home. These presents were highlights of our existence. We didn't get a lot of opportunities to get new clothes, Christmas gifts, and occasional trips to Montgomery Ward. We never had the latest in fashion. While most of our clothes were hand-me-downs, they were clean and well taken care of. That wasn't always good enough for some of the kids at school, however. I remember at least two instances when friends of mine remarked about my clothes being out of style. This hurt me very much. I made up my mind as a teenager that I would always do my best to dress well and be up-to-date.

THE BIRDS AND THE BEES

Naturally, with fifty kids, half of whom were junior and senior high students with hormones running wild, sex education was more hands on than in most homes. We always said we learned anatomy by the Braille system.

There was a fire door separating the teenage boy's and girl's dorms, with a fire bell attached. One evening, we got smart and drilled a small hole in the door so we could get a view of the girls on the other side. I was first to peek. "When what to my wondering eyes should appear," but my own sister. The joke was on me. The fire door served its purpose. However, they forgot about the windows that overlooked the back porch. The roof of that porch proved to be the pathway to many a teenage boy's manhood. The property the teenager's house was on was a part of the former Dodd School for Boys. There was a barn located on the property, across the baseball field and probably 300 feet from the Henson House. It had at one time been used for horses but empty at the time. This barn also served as a great place for learning about the opposite sex. There was the laundry room, and the boiler room that were unoccupied much of the time. Kids would use these rooms to have sexual encounters. Once in a while, you had to wait in line.

The home definitely discouraged boy-girl relationships, but they were inevitable. There were too many places such as the barn for experimenting, and it was too difficult to keep couples apart. With that many young people, there were always short crushes, and sometimes it was just the hormones in action, but boys and girls sought each other out. Most of the time, these encounters were just one-time events, with no emotional attachments. It was amazing that only two or three girls got pregnant in the time I was at the home. In each of these remote cases, it was a boy from town, not the home, who was the father. The girls, by the way, were sent to yet another home, for unwed mothers.

Some of the teenagers naturally had boyfriends and girlfriends from school. This always caused problems. The home didn't like us going in cars, and many of the school activities were forbidden because we were not allowed to dance. It makes sense that we spent all of our time sneaking places to make out. There was nothing else for us to do. If we had been at a sock hop or a dance, we would have been in public or supervised.

ADULT-CHILD RELATIONSHIPS

With the number of kids who went through the home, there were a wide variety of personalities. Most of these were normal, healthy kids with some emotional scars, some smarter than others, some were bullies, some were meek; but all were unique in how they played the hand that was dealt to them.

With the kinds of news stories and headlines we see today, I find it quite amazing that there were not cases of child molestation at the home. Maybe there were, and we just didn't hear about it, but I doubt that. With so many kids, there were very few secrets, and there was always someone who would report most anything they heard to one of the houseparents or social workers. Maybe there were incidents, and they were covered up. From time to time, there were accusations by a teenage girl that a male houseparent had touched her in an improper manner, but nothing serious came of it.

Naturally, with ten to fifteen teenagers living under one roof, there were many romances and a lot of sexual dalliances. A lot of the sex was experimental and normal youthful learning experiences. However, there were some girls with a background of sexual experience and exploitation. They made life more interesting for the teenage boys. I am sure that some of these girls' experiences, unfortunately, had come at the hands of the wrong people, including relatives and individuals who should have been trusted. I do remember instances where teenage girls had crushed on houseparents and times when some of the girls attempted to seduce a male houseparent. These incidents had to be very difficult for the houseparents at the time.

There was one girl who had had an affair with a local barber. The man used to sneak into the main building at night where the girl was a night supervisor for elementary age girls. This girl had some real problems emotionally, and I understand. She has had several failed marriages.

Recently, I had occasion to read through my personal file from the home. One report was from a resident social worker. In my estimation, the report wasn't all that kind to me. However, that is not the reason I am relaying this story. This man seemed to take a very special interest in one teenage girl. This girl was rather well developed and attractive for her age. Debra was actually my first love interest and a very bad influence for me. One night, her and another girl snuck into our dorm, and we spent time in bed together. I was in the seventh grade at the time. One of the other boys squealed about the incident, and we were punished. Debra was one of those girls who had to have a boyfriend wherever she was and had a way of selling herself to most any boy or man she desired. Additionally, she was sexually experienced and had a strong appetite for affection. The social worker was married and had children. Somehow, and I'll never understand why this was allowed, the girl was allowed to leave the home and live with the man's family. I have heard rumors from some of the other girls from the home about this man.

The executive director and his wife took in another teenage girl, who had her share of discipline problems at the home. I do not mean to imply that there was any sign of impropriety because there was not, but while living with the executive director, the girl became pregnant, and the father was one of my classmates. She and the boy did marry and later divorced. This was a great embarrassment for the director and his wife but probably provided a great life lesson for them.

These situations really bothered me personally. About the time both these girls were taken in by people from the home, I wanted badly to be adopted or to go into a foster home. I felt I really needed individual attention and had some talents that could be utilized by my living in a smaller, more nurturing environment. I was very resentful at this time and went through a period of adjustment that wasn't all that healthy for me.

Perhaps I had lived in this institutional environment long enough. Maybe I just wanted individual attention. Whatever the case, I felt I had been overlooked and deeply resented it. I seemed to get along so well with adults and people who invited me into their homes. To this day, I don't understand why I never got the opportunity to live in a foster home as a teenager.

HOMES AWAY FROM HOME

The day I was taken from my parent's home, I was taken directly to the home of Bob and Doris Purtill. They lived in a second floor apartment on at 631 S. Jefferson Ave. in Auburn, Illinois. It was a two-story house with apartments up and down. The house was a darker blue color. It had a porch on the front of the house and two porches in back. There was no garage, but there was a gravel parking area behind the building.

My foster experience was pleasant. My parents weren't mean or abusive like a lot of the people who were foster parents at homes that other kids talked about at the children's home. Mr. Purtill worked in a factory. I remember that he was a smoker, like most everyone at that time. He had diabetes and had to give himself shots daily. Mrs. Purtill did not work outside the home. I recall that she seldom wore anything but her bathrobe and watched an awful lot of TV. She liked to go to matinee movies at the Paramount Theater in downtown Auburn and would sometimes take me along. I remember seeing **The King and I** with Yul Brenner. I also remember a movie with Richard Boone, as a cowboy who froze to death.

My sister, Colleen, lived with the Purtills for a while when I was there, but I really cannot remember anything about our mutual time together. Colleen apparently lived there a lot longer than I did. I was there about six months, while Colleen was a year at least.

I don't have a lot of memories about my stay with the Purtills. I attended school at C. M. Bardwell, an elementary school right down the block. The school is still there. I recalled falling and cutting my arm one day while running home from school. I still have the scar on my right arm. I remember seeing the school crossing guards, who were older and wore uniforms. I thought I might like to be a crossing guard one day.

I was a bed wetter until the fourth grade. Apparently, my problem caused real consternation for those around me and anyone attempting to care for me. The Purtills worked hard at trying to cure me of this bad habit.

Perhaps the bed wetting was a reason that they did not keep me longer. I distinctly remember one episode.

Mr. Purtill and I were at the drugstore one evening. No doubt for drugs for his wife, who my sister believed was a hypochondriac. I saw a pair of guns, with gun belt and holsters as well, that I just had to have. Mr. Purtill promised me that if I could go one week without wetting my bed, he would buy me the set of guns. Miraculously, I did it. Mr. Purtill kept his word and bought me the prize. I was so excited that I wet the bed that night. I don't recall Mr. or Mrs. Purtill's reaction, although I am sure they were sorely disappointed. I was to continue wetting my bed for another three years! I later learned that the main reason for bed wetting was emotional.

From time to time, I had the opportunity to spend some time away from the home with normal families. When I was in the second or third grade, I spent Christmas Day with a local family, the Morrises. It was a great day. I received nice presents, had a great dinner, and enjoyed the life of a normal family. I have remained friends with the family members all of my life, although I was never invited back to their house. I never quite understood that because they were always very friendly to me and I got along with their children.

In the fifth grade, I spent a two-week summer vacation with the Bergfields in Tuscola, Illinois. They were nice people and lived on a farm. I don't remember a lot about the vacation. I do remember that I got a huge boil on my arm while I was there, and we made homemade ice cream nearly every night. They took me to the stock car races. I had never been to a stock car race, and I really enjoyed it. Their daughter, Bobbie, was my age, and we attended college together years later at Brownsville College. Her parents looked me up on the first day of school, and we had a nice cordial visit.

When I was in the sixth grade, a family from the local church took an interest in me. The family had two daughters. The family attended our church and sometimes helped out at the home as houseparents. Maybe it was because Don didn't have a son that he and his wife showed a fondness for me. I was elated that I might have the chance to leave the home and have an opportunity to live the life of a teenage boy in a normal setting with parents and two sisters, instead of forty-five brothers and sisters and intermittent parents. I was allowed to visit their home, and I was aware of their intention to possibly take me into their home. For some reason, which I never found out, the situation never materialized. I don't know if it was their decision or the Kane County Court's decision, but I know that Don told me himself, and he seemed very sad about it. I know I was sad. Maybe the court decided it wouldn't be good to separate me from my four sisters, although I would only be living about a mile away. Maybe the Lawrences felt I was too close in age to their daughters. Whatever the reason, I was disappointed. Shortly after this time, the family moved to another community about forty miles away. I felt close to the Lawrences and they seemed to have a fondness for me as well. Mr. Lawrence in particular seemed upset that the situation did not work out.

I really messed up my next opportunity. Sometime around the age of twelve or thirteen, I had the opportunity to spend some short periods with another local family. They lived in Butte Estates, a small unincorporated area by Burnside that was known for its wealth. The Starcks had a lot of money. They lived in a huge house, (now a bed and breakfast), and raised and raced horses. They took a real interest in me, buying me expensive toys and nice clothes. They invited me to their home several times. They had two children of their own, a boy and a girl. The boy was my age, and the girl was a couple of years younger. For some reason, their son, Jamie, and I didn't get along. While visiting their home as a guest, I got into a fight with Jamie and beat him up. Needless to say, I wasn't invited back. Until the father died about thirty years ago and the Mrs. moved away, they were always friendly and seemed sincere in their inquiries about my well-being. I don't think their son ever forgave me. He always avoided me in school, and I am sure he discouraged his parents from showing any further interest in me.

In the short time I was associated this family, they were very kind to me. I had an hernia operation, and they stopped by the hospital and brought me a couple of nice outfits from the finest clothing store in town. At Christmas, they bought me a gasoline-powered airplane. I've never been very mechanical. I got some gas, started it up, and immediately crashed it into a telephone pole. I was very disappointed to say the least. Maybe, that is one of the reasons I never took further interest in anything mechanical, which I regret to this day.

My fondest memory of any family I visited was the Rook family—Don; his wife, Lois; and daughters, Linda and Judy. They lived in Huntersville, about twenty miles from Burnside. Apparently, they had heard through a friend that a child could be taken from the home for a visit. Being the kind people they were, they felt this could be a reciprocal opportunity for them and a child. Their thinking turned out to be correct. We enjoyed each other very much.

I was thirteen. The mother was to pick me up on Friday afternoon, two days before Christmas, and take me with them for the Christmas holidays. She showed up about 4:00 p.m. We hit it off right away. She was short, round, and always smiling and laughing. She could have been Mrs. Santa Claus. She physically had a resemblance and definitely had the right kind of heart. Despite her short stature, she drove a big 1959 Oldsmobile Catalina. The car was very long, and she had to pull the seat up nearly to the windshield to see. We both enjoyed the ride back, and neither one of us having problems communicating.

Their home was on Edwards Avenue, not far from the local high school. The house was a three bedroom, one bath ranch. It was painted red and was well maintained. When I entered the house, I could immediately feel the warmth, not the temperature, but the warmth of a family that loved and cared about one another. I met Carol, my age, and Judy, three years younger. In a while Lois left to pick Don up at work. Don worked at a local metal spinning company where he had for many years. Upon their return, I was surprised to see a man with a striking resemblance to Don Blocker, who played Hoss on Bonanza. Don was a large man with a big smile, and we hit it off at once.

I have always had a large appetite. Don found this very amusing. Whatever meal we ate, the topic of conversation usually came around to the volume of food I could consume. This got to be a real family joke. I think it made me eat even more, and with Lois only having two girls, she wasn't used to feeding a teenage boy, especially one growing the way I was at the time. I recently contacted the Rook's, and we had dinner. Naturally, my appetite again was one of the dinner topics.

I didn't find out until sometime later, but a very amusing thing happened during my first visit with these fine people. When Mrs. Rook called the home to arrange for the visit, she was told to expect a thirteen-year-old boy. She went out and purchased some toys she thought would be appropriate. When she saw me, she knew she had made a mistake. I was very big for my age and mature beyond my years. I guess she was frantic. She had one day to find alternative gifts for this man-child of a guest. She looked through my clothes to find out my sizes. Knowing I would be attending church and assuming some dressy occasions, I brought white dress shirts along. At the home, all of our clothes were marked with our initials to identify each child's clothes from another's. For some reason, my shirts were marked **band**. When Lois checked out my clothes, she thought the only shirts I had were my shirts used for band at school. I wasn't even in the band. She then bought me a couple of very nice shirts from Ackeman's a fine department store in Elgin. I later also learned that they wouldn't buy their own clothes there but were kind enough to treat me. The family and I have enjoyed laughing at this incident many times since. It is definitely my favorite Christmas story.

The Rook's and I were quite close for the next two to three years. I spent a weekend a month with them. I met a lot of their friends and relatives. I attended funerals and family events with them. In fact, I sang at Lois's mother's funeral and at Carol's wedding. The Rook's came to my voice recital, some of my ball games, and really made me feel like a part of their family. I grew very fond of them and wanted very much to be taken into their home on a full-time basis as a foster child or even as an adoptee.

I asked the home's resident caseworker to discuss the matter with them. He did, and much to my chagrin, they said this possibility had never entered their minds. They said they loved having me visit and were very fond of me, but that idea had not been discussed. I was heartbroken. I was sure, in my heart, that they felt the same way about me as I did about their family. I wasn't angry with them, and I never held it against them, but I always regretted not being able to have them as my family.

We kept in touch throughout high school, but not as much. I was busy working at all my part-time jobs and always had a girlfriend, so we just became less close. The summer after my freshman year in college, their daughter, Carol, stopped by the home. She told me her mother had died, and that they had tried to reach me, but was unable to. They had wanted me to sing at the funeral. I really felt bad. I was a little upset with the people at the home that they didn't try to reach me. I didn't see the family a lot after that. I attended both girls' weddings and ran into Carol and Denny occasionally at shopping malls.

A few years ago, Carol was in Burnside at a local store. She asked the lady who owned the store if she knew me. The lady said she knew me very well. Carol left a note with Vanessa, who forwarded it on to me the next day. We have since visited on several occasions. It was great reconnecting with them, and I am so glad I got to see Don a few times before he recently passed away. My association with this wonderful family is one of the happiest memories of my entire life.

While visiting the Rooks, I was introduced to a neighboring family, Doris and Ernie Capetta. Doris had two children of their own, Tom and Lynn, and a foster child named Bonnie. We were all close in age. I became friends with Doris and Ernie and even dated Lynn for a while. I reconnected with Doris and Ernie at Don Rook's eightieth birthday party. Doris and Ernie now live full time in Florida. My wife and I visited them few years ago. It was great to reconnect and see these fine people.

THE CHURCH'S INFLUENCE

My story cannot be told without addressing the influence of the church. The church controlled the Burnside Children's Home. We felt we were prisoners of the church, which dictated rules and regulations for the home. No smoking, no drinking, no dancing, no sports on Sunday, no spending money on Sunday and very limited rules about theater attendance and TV viewing. In fact, when I first came to the home, houseparents would stand in front of the TV whenever an alcohol or tobacco ad was shown. With the church exercising so much control over the home, I guess we shouldn't have been surprised that local church members felt it was their duty to keep an eye on us kids at all times; which, of course, also meant squealing on us. This made it very difficult for us to get into much mischief at school, the church or anywhere around town.

We attended church more than regularly. We were required to attend Sunday school, Sunday worship, and also evening worship each Sunday. Whenever there were any special services such as a revival meeting or a special musical group or missionary came to visit the church, we were required to be there.

There also were extracurricular programs such as Christian Youth Crusaders or CYC for youngsters, FMY for teenagers, choir, etc. We were forced to join some of the activities, encouraged to join others, and actually had the choice to partake of yet others.

There was the annual weekly church camp at Camp Dotson in Ballard, Illinois. The campgrounds were old, dirty and always stifling hot. We were sometimes allowed to spend time at the camp, several days and nights at a time. While there, we took part in bible study, choir, sports and other wholesome activities. There were also some other activities we enjoyed. Every night after the church service, the teenagers would get together and pair off. It was at Camp Dotson that I experienced my first French kiss. It was in one of the cottages where the parents had left the camp for the day.

There was a group of teens from Chicago who got us together and we had a kissing contest. That was fun. What is also funny is that the girl I paired off with eventually joined the Catholic Church and became a nun. I also made some good friendships at these camps. I met other young people who I would see for several years at other church functions. I met some of them again at Brownsville College. All in all, Camp Dotson brings back fond memories, except for one.

When I was thirteen, I went to Camp Dotson for the day with one of the local church people. While there, I ran into the minister from my home church of Auburn. He invited me to spend the rest of the week with his family. I expected some fun and was bored during the long, hot summer, so I willingly accepted the offer. He called the home and made arrangements. Of course they thought the idea of my spending the next few days with the preacher and his family at the church camp was a splendid one.

There was a hayride that night after the nightly church service. After the event, I found my way to the preacher's cabin. I knocked on the door and was let in by his wife. She and the three children were sitting on the living room floor—all ready for bed. She said I would stay upstairs with her husband. I climbed the stairs and was greeted by the reverend. He too was ready for bed, already in his briefs. He showed me where I would sleep. I would have the double bed, and he would sleep on a cot. I thought that was a bit odd, but I got ready and went to bed. He was busy doing something by the dresser. He started talking to me and explained he slept in the nude. Growing up with so many other children, I was used to seeing other boys naked, but seeing him nude did bother me some.

All of a sudden, he was standing there with an erection! Now I was a little uncomfortable. He sat on the edge of the bed and began reading a French Bible to me. He kept getting closer and would accidentally touch me. Then, very quickly, he put down the Bible and attempted to roll over on top of me. I suddenly realized what was going on. I was very big for my age and was able to push him off. I pulled on my shirt and pants and ran downstairs and out the door as fast as I could go. I looked for places to hide. The church building was locked, while the canteen door was bolted. I couldn't get in the kitchen. I thought about breaking into one of the buildings but didn't have time because I was sure the preacher was going to come looking for me, which he did, but did not find me. Because I had only been at the camp that one day, I didn't know who lived in any of the other cabins. Looking back, I guess I could have knocked on anyone's door and probably gotten help, but I wasn't feeling very trusting at the moment. Finally, I discovered the conference superintendent's car, which was unlocked. I spent the night on the floor of the backseat of a used 1950s era Pontiac, shivering and scared to death. Once during the night, I heard someone walking around. I peeked out the back window and saw the preacher. Luckily, he had his back to the car. In the morning, I went to the conference superintendent and told him the whole story. Apparently, I was not the first young man to report the reverend's behavior. I never testified anywhere, but after several months, he left the ministry and went to work in the library at a major university. Today, I imagine that incident would have made front page headlines, "Local boy from children's home attacked by Preacher!" I am sure the home and the church didn't want any negative publicity, so it all kind of went away. Now that I think about it, I wasn't even interviewed by the home's caseworker about the incident. Maybe that was good. It seems that so many times people have bigger emotional problems after talking about things like this that happened as a child. Maybe it was because I was mature for my age or because I had become hardened to such things or maybe it was because the preacher had not been successful in his attempt to rape me, but the experience has never left me with the kind of damaging emotional scars that so many young people experience after such a thing has happened. I guess I'm just lucky.

Months later, while walking home from school one afternoon, I saw the preacher drive by in his car, heading away from the home. Fortunately, I was within a block of the home. I ran the fastest 300-yard dash in history and secluded myself in my room, with the door locked. The preacher did not attempt to see me, but I think just seeing him scared me more than the actual incident itself.

Another incident happened a few years later that today would cause a stir if I had reported it. The summer after my freshman year at Brownsville College, I worked as an assistant house parent for the elementary age boys at the main building. I slept in a private room between the two dorms. When I think back, I can't believe I was the adult presence in the building at night with twenty-five to thirty youngsters.

At the time, there was also a young, female teacher working as a part-time houseparent, which was very common at the home. We naturally interacted in our jobs. We seemed to get along well. One day, she asked me if I would be willing to go to her apartment that evening to help her move some furniture. Naturally, I was eager to please and agreed. She allowed me to drive her new car to where she lived. She lived in the upstairs apartment of an older house right off of the highway. We went up to her apartment, and she gave me a Coke. I honestly can't remember if I moved any furniture or not. What I do remember is Jane trying to seduce me. She told me she loved me and wanted me to make love to her. I remember her undressing, but I found her unattractive. She was quite heavy. We did not make love, and in my mind, the incident was a nonevent. I did not report it, as I felt it was just a matter between two young people growing up.

I used to think that there were probably no sexual molesters that worked at the home and that houseparents did not make any sexual advances, but now that I am looking at my own situation, I realize that there were two attempts with just myself. I was probably naïve in my thinking.

CRIME AND PUNISHMENT

During the years I resided at the home, corporal punishment was allowed and practiced regularly. I recall being spanked from the time I came to the home until the seventh grade. From seventh grade through high school, I remember being hit by houseparents on occasion.

As younger children, we used to get group spankings for such things as having pillow fights after lights out. Houseparents found it easier to punish everyone rather than try to get someone to admit guilt or to get someone else to squeal. I never objected to being spanked. They only hurt temporarily, didn't last long, and, I thought, were very impersonal. I suppose spanking was a way to deal immediately with a wrongdoing. The houseparent could just take off their belt and give a kid a few whacks right then and there. A lot of times, as time passed, some of the misdeeds were forgotten or forgiven, so I guess spanking took care of the problem right now. Not all houseparents spanked. Some were more creative. I remember one, a former Marine. We stayed up after lights out. He got us up at 5:00 a.m. and made us work all day outside, raking leaves and cleaning up the yard. We certainly slept better the next few nights. Sometimes we were forced to run laps around the football field or were given a specific chore to do. Personally, I thought these kinds of punishment were better than spanking. The exercise was good for the child, and it gave them time to think about what they had done that was wrong.

Punishments were never cruel. Some were more effective than others. Each child reacted differently to his or her punishment. As for me, I always felt I deserved more spankings than I received. Probably, the worst punishment for me when I was younger was being forced to go to bed early. I could never sleep through the night anyway, and going to bed early was torture for me. A favorite punishment the entire time I was at the home was to be kept from eating dinner. I never quite understood that as a punishment. I thought it was rather cruel. Sometimes certain privileges, such as using the telephone, were taken away. Being sent to your room for hours at a time was a way to reprimand. We didn't have televisions or radios in our rooms, and most kids there were not readers, so that made for some pretty boring time. As we got older, there were a lot more kids grounded, which meant we could not leave the grounds except for church and school. This was probably the most effective punishment for the teenagers. You had to be extra careful if you were dating. That made for an easy way for houseparents to punish you for wrong behavior. One of the best punishments I remember is when Reverend Taylor made one teenage boy, Blaine, paint his house after Blaine had run away. He made it all the way to Texas! The punishment was fairly severe, and it saved Rev. Taylor some money and hard work as well. Punishment for crimes committed were a way of life, and we got used to it.

There were hundreds of kids who went through the home—all sizes, shapes, and kinds. Where did they all come from? Why were they there? Most of them came from broken homes, like me. Sometimes the parents were divorced. Often, they were only separated. Most kids didn't stay at the home as long as my family. I think one to three years was an average stay. Most kids came directly from their real homes and also returned after their tenure at the home.

Some kids, however, came to the home directly from other institutions. They came from other children's homes, all-girl or all-boy schools, and not a few of them came from detention homes and/or reform schools. There was a definite difference between these kids, and most of those from private homes. Kids from previous institutions tended to be more hardened and more akin to the ways of the world. Most of the guys already smoked and had been in some sort of trouble. Most of the girls already had sexual experience and had probably been runaways previously. Many of the girls who came to the home as teenagers had come from homes, their own or foster homes, where they had been taken advantage sexually. As a result, many of these girls were sexually active and were willing to share their bodies with boys or even men. They had learned from the wrong adults how to get by in their world. Most of them had also been in trouble, usually for curfew violations or shoplifting. These kids tended to set a bad example and to lead other kids astray. Most young people tend to follow others, and unfortunately, they more often than not follow peers who do wild, unusual, or daring things.

These children from other homes had some pretty scary stories to tell. They were not cared for and cared about like we were at the home. Some of these kids came from homes where beatings happened regularly. Some were even put in cells with buckets for toilets as punishment. Solitary confinement and deprivation of food were not uncommon. It is no wonder that these kids had a bad outlook on life. They felt they had nothing to lose; life had already played a mean trick on them. It was very difficult for houseparents to deal with these kids. Parents know how hard it can be to deal with a teenager of their own, whom they love. One can imagine the stress of trying to reason with those angry, abused young people. It is no wonder that houseparents always had favorites and had kids they were in charge of that they just wanted to give up on dealing with.

There were some ugly scenes at times, like kids running away, skipping school, and having shouting matches with houseparents. These incidents created stressful, heartbreaking times for all of us. Many times when a teen got into a fight with a houseparent, especially if it was a girl, several other kids would join in on the side of the teen, and the fight would become worse. These were the more difficult times to live at the home. There was one occasion when a teenage girl pulled a knife out of her purse and threatened a houseparent. That particular girl was not at the home long after that. She was really one of those rotten apples that spoil the whole barrel. Unfortunately, there were some kids that just could not adjust to life at the home, and they had to be moved elsewhere. This would cause bitterness among the other teens at the time. Although each child tended to fairly self-centered and watched out for themselves, a group dynamic always arose when there was trouble. That kind of scenario always reminded me of watching a prison movie. The inmates got riled up and began to act as a group of prisoners. When the situation got out of control, the houseparents would call other staff in to help quell the situation. Then the entire population of the Henson House would be sent to their rooms, much like a prison lockdown. We were made to be quiet and have a cooling off period. The ringleaders of the incident were dealt with later and usually punished severely for creating a riotlike situation. These kinds of encounters were absolutely the situations at the home that caused me the greatest difficulty. I seldom was able to be on the side of the kids. I was not a troublemaker and liked to have peace at the home. Because of this, a lot of the kids felt angst toward me.

CULINARY DELIGHTS

One thing we always did on a timely basis was eating. Breakfast 6:30 a.m., lunch 12:00 noon, and dinner 6:00 p.m. Not only was dinner always on time, it was also very predictable. The main entrée might have varied, but the format of the meals was always the same. Breakfast was juice, milk, cold cereal, toast; juice, milk, hot cereal; toast, juice, milk, pancakes, toast; juice, milk, French toast, toast. We generally had tomato, orange, or pineapple juice; but occasionally, when money was short, sauerkraut juice was substituted. That was sure a pleasant way to start one's day. Lunch was almost always lunchmeat or peanut butter and jelly sandwiches, which were made the night before by the junior-high girls. On Sundays, we didn't have lunch. We had our dinner at noon, after church. It was always the best meal of the week. We were usually joined by all houseparents, as all age groups ate together in the main dining room. We were also blessed with the presence of the executive director and his family. I suppose that made them feel like they were putting themselves in our shoes. Sometimes, people visiting the church joined us. Dinners generally consisted of your basics. There would be salad, vegetable, maybe soup, meat, potatoes, and dessert. We also had other items very often, namely, macaroni and cheese and frozen fish. To this day, I abhor any type of fish—fresh, ocean, or frozen. We ate a lot of rice dishes too. We ate a lot of food that was donated by other institutions, the government, and companies like airlines. The food was always good and certainly healthy for us. However, I always looked for any reason to eat downtown or in a private home. We never went hungry, and surprisingly, there were never any cases of food poisoning. Meal times were actually kind of a social experience, when all the day's events were rehashed and embellished upon, just like it should be in a real family situation.

MY FAMILY HISTORY

My dad came from a large family, a total of seven boys and seven girls. The family homestead was in the tiny town of Milford, Illinois, with a population of 1,600. I think the sign outside of town still has the same population number on it. The town relied on farming. There was a billboard on Route 1, coming into town, that boasted, "Milford: The Buckle on the Corn Belt." There was also a canning factory in town, which I recall sent off a terrible odor at some times of the year. Most of Dad's brothers and sisters married and had families of their own. The two youngest were not married when we went to the home. My Aunt Mary never did marry. Uncle Syd married about the time I entered high school. Syd and Mary lived at the homestead where they grew up. My grandmother died before I was born, but Grandpa lived with Mary and Sid.

Grandpa was a farmer, and most of the boys followed in his footsteps. They were very hardworking and industrious. Several of the boys stayed in Iroquois County, where Milford was located, and bought farms of their own. They worked hard and played hard. Unfortunately, alcoholism ran in the family. My dad and three brothers were all alcoholics. The effects of their drinking has left a family legacy of heartbreak and problems.

Every summer, Syd and Mary invited us kids down to visit the family farm. Michelle and Colleen generally would go together, and Karen and I would generally go together. After Karen graduated and left the home, I usually would go myself. I liked that best. I don't remember Linda being there as often. I think she spent vacations with our grandmother in Auburn. These vacations were among my happiest childhood memories. Aunt Mary and Uncle Syd treated us very good. They took us to shows, bought us gifts, and took us to visit and meet other relatives. As I am sure is the case in all families, these expeditions left indelible memories. We were exposed to cousins, aunts, and uncles; and I remember sharing some good times with them but never forged lasting relationships with any of them.

My Aunt Mary bowled one night a week. Sometimes after bowling, she would bring a boyfriend back to the house. Looking back, I realize that us being there didn't exactly fit into their plans, but they always tolerated and even amused us. For some reason, Aunt Mary never introduced those guys by name, only as Charlie Black Eye or Charlie Green Shirt. I've always felt very sorry for Aunt Mary. I can't help believe that she missed out on her chance to marry because of her dedication to us kids and her dad. She deserved better. All my life, it was Aunt Mary who had the company at her place. She always arranged family meetings, reunions, and funerals. If there was a family crisis or someone needed help, it was always Aunt Mary to the rescue. Bless her heart!

Uncle Syd was good-natured and fun. We didn't know it as kids, but Syd drank heavily and became an alcoholic. He lost his farm and filed bankruptcy. He got one of his girlfriends pregnant and paid for it with a long and unhappy marriage. Syd and Hazel had two children, Richard and Judy. Judy still lives in the area and helps take care of her dad, but Richard was killed at about the age of twenty in a car accident. Sid let me drive the tractors at a young age and took me with him to the coffee shop every morning. This made me feel very grown up. He tried to teach me to drive, and I drove the pickup truck through a neighbor's fence. I still remember the neighbor's name, Crawford. He also worked me pretty hard on the farm. Baling hay, picking weeds out of soybeans, and detasseling corn were hard, boring jobs; but I felt that I owed him something for all of his and Mary's kindness. One time, while visiting at the farm, I got a terrible sunburn after working all day in the soybean field. Aunt Mary covered my face, arms, back, and neck with vinegar. The sting was gone in the morning.

I have told Aunt Mary and Uncle Syd recently how much their care and generosity meant to all of us as children. I have in the past few years become much closer with Aunt Mary. My wife and I call her a couple of times a month and send her birthday and Christmas gifts. We are really enjoying this, and I know she is too. I hope that our kindness helps in some way to repay all she did for us.

My mom was institutionalized in a state hospital not long after we were taken away. It was several years before I saw her again. I remember my grandma taking Linda, my younger sister, and myself to visit my mom. My grandpa, this was Grandma's third husband, didn't drive, so we took the train or bus to visit. I recall these rides being very boring. The visits were always conducted in an environment that protected Linda and me from the harsh, real world where my mom lived. Grandma Bolden tried hard to keep us kids together and invited us to her house fairly often. She really favored Linda, the youngest, which was probably a good thing as Linda had some real emotional issues from her troubled young childhood.

THE LAST TIME I SAW MY MOTHER

When I was fourteen or fifteen, someone must have decided it would be a good idea for us kids to visit our mom again. By this time, Colleen and Linda had left the home and lived in separate foster homes. My sister Michelle's boyfriend, Larry, also a resident of the home, drove. We were accompanied by our houseparents, Bill and Joan Beebe. We were escorted into a very large room. Actually, the phrase "holding pen" might be more appropriate. It was very scary. There were a lot of sick, deformed, and physically, as well as mentally, disabled people there. Most of them just stared at us like we were the sick ones. One older lady attacked me. She apparently mistook me for her husband or boyfriend and wanted to make love to me. That was very scary.

My oldest sister, Karen, had a bad temper. She felt that the matrons taking care of my mom abused her. An argument ensued, and Karen proceeded to punch out the lady. This naturally caused quite a stir. Between these two events, the day was quite unforgettable. That was the last time I saw my mom. At some point, she was transferred to another state hospital in Illinois. She lived in several nursing homes over the years and died at the age of eighty-one. Sometimes I feel guilty because I haven't seen her, but on the whole, I don't think my decision is entirely wrong. The few times I did visit our mother, all she could talk about was getting her out of the hospital. She wanted to live with us. She wanted us to take care of her. She always wanted money. I knew in my heart that she would never leave this type of controlled environment. I guess I felt this was her lot in life, just as mine was to stay at the home until I graduated from high school. I feel that more pain and heartbreak would be caused for both of us through further contact. I know my mom would never be able to comprehend my reasoning. I hope she can forgive me.

EDUCATION

Most of us were average students. I only remember a couple of kids making the honor roll. First of all, we were a pretty good cross section of the population, and only a small percentage would be in the upper grades of the class. Secondly, we all had come from broken homes, and our emotional states of mind no doubt affected our ability to concentrate, and our attitude toward achievement in any area. The home's official policy was for us to do well in school, but in actuality, I think they really hoped that we passed each grade and didn't cause any problems. They wanted us to make it through high school and then move on. The home had a required study period for one hour each night for us to study and do our homework. Depending upon the individual houseparent, the study periods were successful or merely quiet times. For the high-school-age kids, the home hired local teachers to come in and work as tutors for the study periods. This was helpful to us as students.

Only a few of us went on to college. Naturally, money was a huge issue, even if any of the kids had a desire to go to college. Again, the home paid a lot of lip service to the college idea, but only provided real moral support to a few of us. They were unable to provide any financial aid but helped us apply to schools and apply for whatever financial help might have been available.

A lot of people assume that our classmates ostracized us kids. This was not the case. We were generally accepted by our peers and treated as equals. Of course, there was not a lot of interaction between us and other kids since we weren't able to take part in a lot of extracurricular activities. One reason was scheduling. Whether it was sports, school plays, or whatever, our participation caused a problem for those preparing meals. Meals had to be held over. Any special tasks like this caused a break in the routine, which was a problem for houseparents and those kids doing chores. The others usually resented those of us who were involved in school activities. A little envy, a little jealousy, I suppose. Another reason was that if we became popular with other kids it eventually led to us asking for more privileges. These additional privileges were generally frowned upon—dances, overnight stays, and nonchaperoned dates. Personally, I found it very much to my advantage to be involved in other activities. Whether school, church, or employment, I attempted to project a positive image for the home while I was doing other things. I found this helpful in getting special considerations from houseparents and staff members. This did, however, cause some consternation with the other kids. They referred to me as a PC or privileged character. This was not necessarily an endearing term, as it was generally caused by jealousy. Their attitude hurt me, but I had to take care of myself, especially since I was the one who had been at the home the longest and knew that I would be there through high school while many of the other teens were only there for a short while.

MEDICAL CARE

We received better medical and dental care than most private homes. The professional people who took care of us deserve a lot of credit. I know payment to them was slow. In my own case, all doctor visits had to be approved, and payment came only after bills were submitted to the court. There were also many instances when parents didn't pay bills they were supposed to.

The nursing home, connected with the home, was located across the street. There were nurses and nurses' aides on staff. This became very convenient at times when inoculations such as polio, measles, etc. were necessary. We would simply march across the street en masse and take our medicine. They also had a good supply of over the counter medicines, bandages, and the like. We were always being told to "run over to the manor" if any supplies were needed in case of an injury or cold.

When certain sicknesses like measles, chicken pox, or flu was contracted by one of the kids, it usually spread throughout the home rather quickly. Each building and, when possible, each dorm, had a sick bay area that was usually occupied by someone most of the time. There were times when such illnesses as measles or chicken pox ran rampant through the whole home, and nearly everyone was sick. This really had to be a challenge for the staff, especially if they had children of their own.

There were the usual cases of tonsillitis, appendicitis, and hernias. There were a lot of varied illnesses, but I don't remember any serious problems and no deaths, which I consider pretty amazing when considering the number of children who passed through the home in twelve years I was there. One six-year-old boy did die when he ran in front of a truck and was killed.

There were two particular doctors I particularly remember. Dr. Reese was our dentist. From my experience with him, I learned that the term *dentist* was synonymous with pain. Every time I went there, he hurt me. I'm sure it wasn't intentional because he was really a very nice man and still is. He was always friendly and warm, wanting to know what was going on in our lives. Maybe he just wasn't careful, which I find hard to believe since he has nine children of his own. Whatever the cause, visits to him were very scary; and after I left the home, I didn't go to a dentist for twelve years.

Dr. James C. Dolbert was a local family practitioner. He still made house calls. In my estimation, he was a very good doctor. He always seemed to have the correct diagnosis and seemed to have the right prescription or cure. The only complaint I had about him was that a visit to his office took hours. I learned years later that the reason for this was because he treated everyone, rich or poor, young or old, no matter how much money people owed him and still provided service. He was always quick with a shot of penicillin or a bottle of pills. Years after I left the home, I remember people referring to him as a pill pusher. This saddened me because I felt he was very qualified, dedicated, and compassionate. I even remember occasions when he came to the home to see a sick child. As an adult, I knew several of the nurses that worked for Dr. Dolbert over the years. They spoke very highly of him as a doctor and employer. I wish I could find a physician today like him.

When glasses were needed, we went to Dr. Meister. He was the father of one of my school classmates. He was another nice man who deserves credit for being good to the kids at the home.

EXCURSIONS AND EVENTS

We were very fortunate to get free tickets and passes to a lot of events, like the county fair, carnivals, circuses, ball games, concerts, and local events at schools. Sometimes we were given the option of attending these events, but many times, attendance was required. As one might guess, the required attendance events were not sellouts, so our being there usually helped to fill up the seats. In addition, any event that was of a religious nature required our attendance. Don't get me wrong, we were able to see a lot of things other kids missed, and I'm grateful for that. One time, we were treated to a hotel stay and visit to Mark Twain's home in Hannibal, Missouri. We visited Mark Twain Cave and went spelunking. I remember that I fell into one of the caves and got a bit scratched up.

This was exciting since most of us had never stayed in a hotel before. Another time, we attended a Duke Ellington concert. My roommate and I found that kind of boring and snuck out, which was what happened at many of these events. In the summertime, we were taken to Lake Geneva several times each season to Big Foot Beach. That was always a treat. These excursions had to be stressful for the houseparents, trying to keep track of everyone and know what they were up to. Most times, we went to these events there was some mischief. Kids almost always took off and got caught with someone of the opposite sex, caught smoking or shoplifting. Shoplifting and smoking were the major choices of crime at the home.

Myself, I usually used these events as opportunities to meet new people and make friends. This apparently was a good tactic as I have always been good at networking and using public gatherings as a place to make good contacts for business.

THE VILLAGE

The village was the "old people's home," as stated on the sign out front. "Burnside Homes referred to the Children's Home and the Village." While my story is about the Children's Home, it would not be complete without including some commentary about the Village.

As I stated earlier in the book, The Village was where we got our basic nursing and medical care, as they had full-time nurses on staff. Some jobs were provided for us by the Village, such as washing dishes, nurse's aide, doing laundry and yard work.

The manor, as we referred to it, sat across the street, Park Street, from the Children's Home. It was a huge building. Red brick colored with white window trim, it sat prettily along the highway. I don't recall exactly how many rooms there were, but I would estimate thirty private rooms. Some of these had one person to a room, and some had two people in a room. There was a ward at one end of the building that was more like intensive care. Usually, when someone went to the ward, they knew they were close to passing on. We always hated going in the ward. The odor was bad, and all the people in the beds seemed to be in pain or so uncomfortable.

The manor had a very nice common area where the residents could congregate and watch television. There was a small screened porch attached to that that was furnished comfortably. There was always an activities director that would put on programs and activities for the residents. Many times, us kids were called upon to sing for the old people. I enjoyed doing that. The kitchen and executive offices were located in the basement of the building.

Beyond the main building of the manor, there was a group of buildings that were used for independent living. One building had four apartments, and then there were two duplex units. There was a nice lawn area where the residents could sit outside. There was also a hill on the back side of the building that we used for sledding and tobogganing. At the bottom of the hill was an area that would collect water, and we used that for ice skating in the winter time. Across the parking lot sat a very large old Victorian home that was used as apartments for staff members. My friend, Cliff, lived in one of the apartments with his parents.

To the north of the manor, sits the church. The church was built in the 1950s and was a pretty modern design for the times. It still looks good today. It is one story, L-shaped, with very pretty multicolored windows.

The entire compound of the Children's Home, the manor, and the church took up about a four-square block area. Today the Children's Home is gone, but the manor has grown, and the day care facilities have expanded, so the same areas are occupied.

EASTER

It was a very religious holiday, and I remembered that attending church services was not only required, but we seemed to have to dress up more, and the occasions seemed more somber somehow. I remember that the church always had Easter lilies decorating the church on Palm Sunday. We were off school on Good Friday and were required to attend a special service at noon at the church. Businesses in town closed down from noon to 3:00 p.m. in honor of Good Friday. Easter Sunday must have been an important day. The church was always full with people, and everyone was more dressed up than usual. In those days, people wore dresses and suits and ties to church, but on Easter Sunday, everyone seemed to have on something new or special.

Leaving church, I would hear people talking about where they were going for dinner. It seemed that either everyone was going someplace special, or they were going to have a houseful of company. Some people talked about going out for brunch. I had never been to a brunch as a child and didn't quite know what that was, but it sounded like they were looking forward to it. The home would put on a very nice dinner for Easter Sunday. I think we generally had ham as the main course, which was a treat. We had all the extra trimmings to go with it. There always seemed to be people at the dining room table reserved for guests on Easter Sunday. Maybe these people were traveling and knew they could get a nice free meal.

Easter to us kids mainly meant Easter vacation. Today, I think it is just referred to as spring break, with the religious connotation removed from the equation. I think that is sad. Some kids would go to their real homes or to relatives for the week, but I was usually at the home. As a youngster, this was pretty boring. There was not much to do with a lot of kids gone, and the weather still wasn't very nice outside. As a teenager, the week of Easter vacation was better. I had friends to hang with in my early teens; and as a high school student, I was usually working. Whenever we had a break from school, I made sure that I had somewhere to work to earn extra money and also to keep myself occupied.

HOUSEPARENTS AND STAFF

Betsy Lampkin. Ms. Lampkin was young, pretty, and strict. She was my first houseparent. She wasn't there too long. She married a man from the local church and moved away.

Nona Rogers. Ms. Rogers was my next houseparent. She was nice and took a real interest in me. In reviewing my personal file, I found her comments about me interesting. I think she had very good insight into my personality.

Margaret Garrett. Ms. Garrett was young and single. She was trained as a nurse. She took me home to her parent's house one weekend in Freeport, Illinois. She was a very nice lady. I ran into her in Burnside about the time I was forty years old. She was married and looked much the same. She still lived in Freeport.

Beatrice Hester. Beatrice stayed at the staff house with her daughter, Shiela. Beatrice was the laundry lady. I used to talk to her for long periods while she ironed. She taught me how to iron, and I have done my own ironing all my life. My wife recently gave me a fancy new iron for Father's Day—my male friends got a real kick out of that. Her daughter now lives in Rockford, Illinois, and is a social worker.

Dianna Cutler. Ms. Cutler was my sister's first houseparent. She was young, single, and a lovely person. She stayed for several years. She married a local man and always stayed close to the home. She worked as a part-time houseparent for many years. She had a soothing, caring way about her. She always made you feel good. She always was very concerned about the kids in our family. She still lives in Burnside. I saw her often as an adult. Ms. Cutler was one of those people you describe as "She was a saint."

85

Marvin and Tina Gates. They were a young married couple. Tina's parents worked at the manor where her dad, a retired minister, was the administrator and her mother was the cook. Her brother, Cliff, was my best friend. Martin was an ex-Marine. He had two important influences on me:

1. Encouraged me to be involved sports.
2. Helped me to control my temper.

Martin was a stern and good disciplinarian. He made the "punishment fit the crime." I liked his organized and regimented style. Tina was spoiled, immature, and jealous. She got very pouty when she didn't get her way. They moved back to Kansas, and I believe I heard they eventually divorced. I was fond of the whole family.

Oscar and Jennifer Diener. The Dieners hailed from Nebraska. They had two children, Tom and Mary. While working as houseparents, Oscar attended Whiston College. He was studying to be a social worker. I was very close to Oscar. He taught me how to tie a tie. He encouraged my participation in little league. He was a big baseball fan, so I got to watch Cub's games with him and his son. The Dieners both gave me a lot of special attention. He was probably the best role model for me the whole time I was at the home. I was broken hearted when they left. If the Dieners would have stayed at the home and I would have always been under their care, I think my life would have turned out differently. I think I would probably have become a preacher because of their strong influence. Jennifer Diener visited the home one Sunday when I was in high school. She looked me up, and we visited. She told me that Oscar had died and told me that he was always very fond of me and wondered about me. I was sad to hear of his death.

Karl and Mona Bailey. The Baileys were from Burnside. Karl had worked for many years as a carpet and floor installer for a local retailer from our church. When his knees could not take it anymore, they came to work at the home. They had a daughter, Laverne. They were very caring people, but not good role models for me. They cared little about their appearance. They were sloppy and uneducated. Don't get me wrong. They were good people and really cared about the kids. They were probably better houseparents for most of the kids because they were not as religious and knew more about what life was really like. I know they liked me, and I liked them too. I always felt that Karl felt badly that he and I didn't have more in common. To help financially, Karl sold Amway, and Leona sold Mary Kay. While they probably didn't keep the Henson House up to the cleanliness standards the home wanted, I think they probably had one of the more stress-free environments of all the houseparents.

Dawn Klingberg and Marie Thigpen. These ladies were trained as teachers. They served as houseparents for the teenagers for a time. We didn't know it at the time but later learned that they were a lesbian couple. Perhaps that is why they didn't stay at the home long. They remained in Burnside, their house was on my paper route, and taught in local schools.

Mr. and Mrs. Highsmith. This couple wasn't at the home too long. I think he was finishing up his master's degree or something like that. Nice young couple. Mr. Highsmith had a withered arm, but that didn't keep him from playing sports with us. I think they did a nice job with the younger boys.

Mr. and Mrs. Brown. They were from Ohio. They were older than most houseparents. Mr. Brown had worked as a prison guard, and he always sat around with one of those hand exercising things. They were kind of cranky and not right for the job. They had a hard time relating to the kids and didn't last long.

Carole Buscher. Carole was young and single. Her parents owned a farm in Burnside, and they attended our church. I remember when I was in the third or fourth grade, I had a temper tantrum over something and let out a bunch of swear words. Ms. Buscher spanked me and wrote up a report that said I could "swear like a truck driver." I have no idea where I learned that language. She married a local man, the son of Bart Hurst, a home employee. She was good houseparent despite her young age.

Paul Junger. Paul was a social worker. He was young and seemed very sincere. He was good for me to communicate with. He was a good listener, and you felt that you could trust him. His wife, Jeanette, was very pleasant. She was a music major and played the piano at our church. Paul and I sang duets. He encouraged me to pursue music and college. Paul and his wife moved back to Ohio. He has worked at a mental health facility for forty years. I recently called him. He had a pretty good memory about my family and the home.

Clinton Taylor. Mr. Taylor was the executive director when I came to the home. He was a minister. I never felt that he was a real good administrator. He seemed more interested in promoting himself. He took advantage of the home financially. I remember he took the home on trips that others felt were for the benefit of his own kids. He eventually became an English teacher and then principal at Burnside High School, where he retired. Mr. and Mrs. Taylor had three children of their own. Cindy, the daughter, was the oldest. Clint was two years older than me, and Larry was my age. All three children later attended Brownsville College where I was a fellow student with Mike and Larry for a year. I liked Reverend Taylor better after he left the home. He became a lot more friendly to me later on when I became active in politics. I do recall one specific interaction with him as a child. One night during dinner, I was called into his office. He very nicely told me that if I didn't quit wetting my pants and my bed, they would have to send me to a different home to live. I guess he was trying a new psychology with me. I'm not sure if it had a direct effect or not, but I remained at the home for another seven or eight years.

John and Lilly Keating. Reverend Keating was the executive director of the home. He came in 1959. He had been a minister in New York, where he had a reputation for working well with youth. He and Lilly had two children, Jake and Donna. Donna is now a doctor. Lilly was a music major. John was a good administrator and business manager. He was fair and a very caring man but didn't have good rapport with kids. Mr. Keating was bald, and kids referred to him as Chrome Dome and Bald Mouse. Lilly taught summer school classes. She played piano and organ at church. The longer and better I got to know the Keatings, the better I liked them. Most people didn't realize it, but Mr. Keating had a real good sense of humor. Kids at the home didn't like Jake and Donna. They were too studious and shy, plus we were all a little jealous of all houseparent's children just because they had a happy home. During Reverend Keating's administration, it became obvious that the Burnside Children's Home, as it had always been operated, was an anachronism, a thing of the past. The State of Illinois would not send children and money to the home if the religious rules were to be enforced, and the home couldn't really survive without the funding. If the home was going to survive, it would need to expand the operation of the Manor Nursing Home. In addition to expansion of the nursing home business, the Burnside Homes opened a day care facility, which has become a successful operation over the years. The original children's home building was razed, and that property is now part of the manor operation. The day care center was built on the old Dodd School for Boys' football field. All of this was done during Reverend Keating's administration. I just recently learned that Reverend Keating passed away. I was saddened. I wish I had the chance to express to him what a great job he did at the home.

Georgia Johnson. For as long as I remember, she was the administrative secretary to the executive director. Georgia and her husband, John, had two children, Pam and Nick. Georgia was strict but nice. I always got along well with her. Some of the kids were afraid of her because they thought she tattled everything to Mr. Keating. I don't know if that was true.

Vern and Melissa Trinton. They had three children—Terri, Pam, and Peter. They were both teachers and had come from Kansas. They were houseparents for the teens at the Heston House, and later, Mr. Trinton held some kind of administrative position at the home. They were conservative and strict. They worked hard at whatever they did. The Trinton's were very religious and adherent to rules. They seemed to have a real problem with couples and discouraged boy-girl relationships. Mr. Trinton was a believer in corporal punishment and was not afraid to practice it. Mr. Trinton always drove big, fancy used cars. They eventually left the home. He taught at Burnside High School and retired from there. They have probably done the best job of staying in touch with kids from the home of any houseparents. They were also probably the most respected, even if not best liked set of houseparents. Their son, Peter, became a minister. Their children have raised nice families of their own.

I recently have been in touch with Georgia Johnson and Melissa Trinton. Sadly, both of their husbands have died. They live in the same retirement complex, the Light and Life Home, in Lakeland, Florida. This is a retirement complex operated by the church. I should visit there. There are probably other people I would know from the home and church.

Amy Postma. Amy was a college student. She came from Iowa, had pretty red hair, and was quite well developed physically. She worked for a year as an assistant houseparent. She was a nice young lady. She used to help me with my schoolwork. I actually had a crush on her for a while. I would guess that she has had a successful career.

Phil Carter. Phil was studying to become a minister. He was from Chicago and attended the Northern Illinois Baptist Theological Seminary in Lombard, Illinois, which I drove by almost daily. Paul was great for us boys to have around. He was tall, nice looking, soft-spoken, and a good athlete. He spent time with us and set a good example for us.

Phil and Lynn Newman. Phil and Lynn were very unusual houseparents. They started working at the home as tutors during study hall. Lynn was a teacher, and Phil worked at a local manufacturing company as a mechanical engineer. Through the tutoring, they found they had a fondness for some of the kids and began houseparenting part-time. They were not at all interested in church or religion. They simply wanted the extra money. The Newmans allowed kids from the home to come to their house. They let us smoke and, heaven forbid, play cards. They were intelligent and a little on the liberal side. They were one of the few houseparents who encouraged us to think and consider alternative opinions. They moved away from Burnside after about a year.

Liz Hampton. Aunt Liz, as she was called, was the cook when I came to the home and continued in that position for several years. She was a single mother. I don't remember if she was divorced or a widow, but she was a great lady. She was always cheerful and kind. Her only child was a son, Wes, who was quite popular at school.

Many Friday nights, she would invite the boys over to her cottage to watch **Shock Theater**. She would fix popcorn for all of us and allow us to just be boys. It was funny. We couldn't wait for these Friday nights to stay up late and watch Frankenstein Meets the Wolf Man, but when the show was over, we were all scared to walk back up to our dorm. I visited my sister one summer in Michigan. I traveled by train with Aunt Liz. That was a nice trip. Aunt Liz was always fun to be around.

Bart Hurst. When I arrived at the home, Mr. Hurst was the maintenance man. He had been a previous executive director and was the father of Mr. Taylor's wife. Mrs. Hurst helped out as the assistant cook. They were both very strict. Bart was downright mean. There were several occasions when he lost his temper and way over reacted to a child's behavior. I recall one time that he got mad at one boy and broke a screen door over his back. I don't remember exactly what the infraction was, but I know it was not major. Another time, he got angry with a teenage girl for the way she was operating the dishwasher and just beat her in front of all of us. It was awful. Another time, he was driving us in the bus, and my sister, Michelle, made him angry. He made her sit in the back engine compartment. She got sick. One of my more memorable experiences at the home involved Mr. Hurst. At age eight or nine, it was my chore each morning to take laundry out to the laundry house. One morning upon my arrival with my load of clothes, I came upon the largest ring of keys I had ever seen. I don't know why, but keys fascinated me. I don't know what possessed me, but I took the keys and started to leave the premises. All of a sudden, he charged out from behind the washing machine and grabbed me. After scaring the hell out of me, he went into a diatribe about why I had stolen the keys. "So you can get into more places and steal more stuff!" Jeez, I was just curious. You would think I had murdered someone, but that's how his temper was. He really made an impression on me. The incident also cured me of any future pilfering.

Dale was the son of Bart Hurst, and one of the more colorful people to be associated with the home. As kids, we all knew of Dale. He attended our church and lived with his parents, being around the home grounds quite regularly. We also knew that he had served time. If I ever knew what he had done, I have forgotten. However, it seemed to me then, (at ten to fourteen years old, and certainly is a fact today, that Dale should not serve as a houseparent. Dale began dating one of our houseparents, Carole Buscher. They eventually married and worked on and off as houseparents. I remember Carole as kind and fair, while Dale as a little rough. He had his dad's temper. The one incident that sticks out in my mind involved a teenaged female runaway. Sue had run away and Dale was sent, alone, to pick her up. I feel this was a bad idea in the first place, but Dale was the houseparent. Upon her return, the girl was angry and very vocal. She claimed that Dale tried to rape her. I don't know for sure, but I think the charge was ignored.

Chester and Melody Flowers were houseparents for a while for the teenagers. Chester was quiet and sort of odd. Mrs. Flower was a pretty lady with a nice singing voice. I never thought they made a good couple and was not surprised to find out they later divorced. I think they had a daughter. After leaving the home, they remained in Burnside.

RUNNING WILD

For many years, kids were not allowed to own any motor vehicles. I can understand their reasoning. There basically was no need for most kids to have a car. Where would they be kept? How would the home keep track of all the kids if they had cars? Everyone knows, of course, that cars are just breeding grounds for trouble with teenagers. It certainly wouldn't look good for homeless kids, partially supported by the community, to have motorcycles or cars when other kids in school couldn't afford them.

Nevertheless, in about 1963, Jeremy Whiston, my future brother-in-law, was allowed to buy a motorcycle. Jeremy was a good, honest, and hardworking kid who caused no problems. He did a lot of odd jobs for people, and transportation was a problem. Rev. Keating decided to take a chance with Jeremy. There were no problems, and Jeremy was eventually allowed to buy a car. His first car was a 1956 four-door Chevy Bel-Air. He eventually bought a really cool 1961 burgundy Chevrolet convertible. It had a 409 engine, really sharp car! Since he was madly in love with my sister, I got to ride in it a lot.

I too was allowed to have a vehicle. I bought a Honda motorcycle during my junior year in high school. I have the receipt, which was in my personal file from the home. The agreement made rules I was to obey regarding operation of the cycle. If I broke the rules, I would be forbidden to ride the bike for thirty days. I needed the bike for work as I worked several different part-time jobs during my junior and senior years at diverse locations throughout the town. I enjoyed the bike very much. It gave me a lot of extra freedom and little social status as well. Two of my friends and I bought bikes together one night after school. We would meet up every morning and ride together. You would have thought we were the hell's angels or something. I obeyed traffic regulations and Rev. Keating's rules until one Sunday evening following church services. For some silly reason, I ran four stop signs along Madison St. This wasn't bad enough. A cop followed me all four blocks. When Rev. Keating saw my name in the paper, I lost the privilege of operating my cycle for thirty days, as agreed to in the form I signed. It was a long month without my bike. I did learn two valuable lessons from this experience. Number one, Rev. Keating meant what he said; and number two, get a rear view mirror! Having the Honda and being able to work at so many places allowed me freedom but also caused me sadness because I saw how other people lived, and it made me want a home of my own.

MY FIRST LOVE

I moved to the Heston House for high schoolers after seventh grade. Moving there was a big deal. You were with high school kids and got more privileges. It is strange how this **privilege** came about. I was infatuated with a girl at the home, definitely my first love. She was very pretty and was physically very well developed for an eighth grade girl. She had already been sexually active and was very affectionate. She did not hold back with her feelings. One night, she and another girl snuck into our dorm. Tina was with me, in my bed, and Chris was with one of the other boys. One of the other boys, apparently out of envy, squealed. The home decided I was a little too mature to be with my own age group, and I was allowed to move in with the older kids. This was the greatest punishment I had ever received in my life. Tina caused me some problems. I was willing to break rules to be with her. That same summer, I visited a family, the Youngers, in Batavia for a two-week period. Mr. Younger reminded me of Fred McMurray on *My Three Sons*. I had a nice time there. They had a daughter a little older than me, and there were a lot of kids coming and going. Tina was visiting with her brother and sister in Elgin, just a few miles away, and called to see if her brother and sister could pick me up and take us to the show. This was allowed. Unfortunately, I didn't get home until two o'clock in the morning and really worried the Youngers. They called the home and reported it. They were told, "Andy is a really good kid, but if he is going to get into trouble, it will be with Tina." I broke up with a very nice girl from town who was very popular at school. This did not bode well with some of the kids from school, although some of my guy friends were envious because Tina was really quite a sexy girl.

THE RESIDENTS

This wouldn't be a good story without telling about some of the kids. I have mentioned anecdotes about specific kids, but a few lines about others will help to give a flavor for life at the home. Some of the stories will only relate to their time at the home. Some of the others will tell what I know of what happened to them after their departure from the home.

Wilhemina came to the home at the age of about thirteen, a year older than me at the time. She apparently came from an abusive home, both physically and sexually. Her sisters were older, and she apparently looked up to them and wanted to do whatever they did, whether right or wrong. Wilhemina, or Willie as she preferred to be called, was starved for attention. She would do anything for anyone who would befriend her. She was especially fond of my sister, Michelle. Willie followed her around like a puppy dog. Michelle tried to be her friend, but it was a very trying experience for her. Willie would wear out her welcome by being too complimentary and constantly performing favors even when the favors weren't desired. Wilhemina also attached herself to some kids at school and also wore out those friendships. Certain individuals, usually attractive girls who were definitely out of her league, enamored her. She would, in today's parlance, stalk these people. She would phone them, write them, and harass their friends, families, and lovers. She really became a nuisance to those she liked. To those she didn't like, Willie was a gossip, pest, and a vindictive and conniving teenage girl who was always in the midst of people with problems. To those not directly involved with her, she was simply amusing. After leaving the home, Willie married an older man from town. I think she had a baby with him.

Mac came to the home at about the age of twelve or thirteen, a couple of years younger than me at the time. I don't know if Mac had any brothers or sisters or why he was placed in the home. I do know, however, that Mac had serious problems. He had a bad temper, didn't like authority, and seemed to have a death wish. He was always doing some daredevil act, two of which eventually caught up with him. I'm not sure at exactly the age, but I think about fifteen, Mac was doing laundry for the home as a part-time job. There was a large commercial washing machine and a large commercial dryer, separated by a machine called an extractor, which spun the water out of the clothes before going into the dryer. This machine spun extremely fast, and one afternoon, Mac decided to see just how fast by sticking his arm into the machine while it was running. He did. The extractor pulled his arm right off. Attempts were made to save the arm, but eventually, it was amputated, and Mac was given a prosthesis. Later in life, Mac was killed in an auto accident at a fairly young age. I don't know the details of the accident, but I am aware that his driving habits reflected his other daredevil antics.

Derek was one or two years younger than me. He had two younger sisters, Lana and Nancy. I don't know whatever became of Derek, but anyone who remembers him remembers his constant loud threat, "I'm gonna blow this place up." He was totally harmless, and Lana was a very sweet girl. I don't remember much about Nancy, as she was quite a bit younger.

Lenny came to the home in the sixth grade and stayed through high school. He was in my grade at school, and we had some classes together. Lenny always had trouble adjusting. He was a loner and was always indifferent to others. One thing I recall about Lenny was that he was caught, on more than one occasion, being mean to animals, a definite sign of a sick individual. No one liked Lenny, and we were all guilty of picking on him. After high school graduation, Lenny returned to his hometown with his family. By the time he was twenty-one, Lenny had hanged himself. I felt bad when I heard this since I never gave Lenny a chance. I've tried as an adult to be more understanding and compassionate of people less fortunate, especially ones with obvious emotional problems.

Dennis was one of five children: Dennis, Bill, Deb, Tom, and Jerry. They came from Chicago. All the kids were a little fast for the rest of us, obviously having been exposed to more of life than we were. They were also a very good-looking bunch of kids. Their mom had dated a former major league baseball player for a while. They had a lot of stories to tell. I believe a fair number of them were just that—stories—but their lives had definitely been more exciting and colorful than most of ours. Later, I heard that their mom had been a prostitute, but I don't know that for a fact.

Dennis was a bit diabolical. He had everything going for him. He was smart, very good-looking, and a star athlete. Dennis was very popular with the guys and the girls. Dennis was about a year older than me, but we were in the same grade. We played sports together—baseball, football, and basketball. We were both starters, but somehow Dennis was always a little bit better than I. I was jealous of him, but we always remained very good friends. Our girlfriends were best friends. We lied to cover up for each other, and even fought other guys on each other's behalf. However, Dennis had another side. I guess it was that big city attitude. He always wanted to be on the edge of trouble, if not directly involved in it. I began to see that Dennis and I would end up in trouble if we continued to hang around together. It was about this time that the whole family of five left the home. A friend I met at church camp and that I had kept in touch with for years, told me several years ago that Dennis had been arrested for car theft. What a waste. Dennis was a young man with all the basics, and more, to succeed in life but always wanted more excitement. Life on the edge had finally won and pushed him over to the wrong side.

Dustin liked to refer to himself as "Dustin James Debowe." You had to hear him pronounce it to really appreciate it. Dustin had a twin sister, Desiree. They fought constantly, like most twins, and were as different as night and day. They came from Burnside. Their dad was a local carpenter who worked too little and drank too much. I don't recall if the parents were divorced or what their situation was, but like my family, Dustin and Desiree spent many years at the home. Dustin was probably one of the brightest kids to ever go through the home. He was one of the few to make the honor roll. For a child, Dustin was eccentric. He liked classical music, read more adult style magazines, and dressed too old for his age. Dustin amused us all, and we had good times making fun of him, but it was all in good fun.

I don't remember what prompted it, but one evening, when most of the kids were gone somewhere, me and my roommate broke into Dustin's locked footlocker. He was way too protective and secret about that footlocker, and we needed to know why. We found a collection of Playboy Magazines, cigarettes, and even a half pint bottle of rye whiskey. It was like we had discovered gold! We were mostly surprised by the Playboys since us guys often wondered if Dustin was gay. Dustin went on to college and became a fifth-grade teacher.

More about Desiree, Dustin's twin sister. She was giddy, very boy crazy, and quite likable. She was a good student and a responsible young girl. She had one problem. She was what I would refer to as a nymphomaniac. While I am no expert at defining the term, I know that she was sexually active as a teen, mostly with older men, and it seemed that she couldn't resist any man's advances. In fact, I understand that she usually was the one making the advances. One evening, while I was helping to supervise the younger boys, Desiree asked me if I could help her move some furniture in the attic. As always, I wanted to be helpful. We went to the attic. There was an old bed there, with a mattress on it. I asked if that was the furniture she wanted moved. She didn't say anything. She just took her clothes off and pulled me onto the bed. That was the only time Desiree and I interacted like that. Nothing was ever said about it afterward. As an adult, I understand Desiree has had multiple relationships with men, mostly unsuccessful. I don't know what her current situation is. I don't know what Dustin and Desiree's relationship is today, but I know they didn't communicate for years, allegedly because of Desiree's promiscuity and problems with men.

Chenoa was my age. We had a lot of classes together and had some mutual friends. Chenoa was a very nice, bright girl. She was part Native American and definitely looked like it. I think I remember her having a younger sister at the home. Chenoa was well liked at school and by kids at the home, as well as by houseparents. She was a good student and had musical talents. She was one of the other teens beside me who sang and performed for other churches and community groups on the home's behalf. Chenoa was also quite a talented artist. She went on to college and became a nurse. I always knew she would be a success.

Skins was my best friend from the home. He was a year older but in my class in school. At some point, Lonny had been held back a year at school. He had siblings, but they did not come to the home. Lonny's stay at the home was pretty unremarkable. He came here while in eighth grade and stayed through high school graduation. Lonny was tall, skinny, and had a couple of front teeth missing. However, Lonny was well liked by all of us. He was very shy which kept him from doing real well at school. Lonny gave no one any trouble, including houseparents and staff. He would do anything for anyone, but never one to do much for himself. While Lonny didn't seem outstanding at the home, in my estimation, he sure did well afterward. He went into the Army after high school and on to Vietnam. When he returned a few years later, we could no longer refer to him as "Skins." He had filled out, muscled up, and gained self-confidence. I felt proud of him. Lonny was best man at my first wedding, and I have remained friends with him and his wife ever since. He is now a proud grandfather and a sergeant in the Burnside Police Department. We are all proud of Lonny.

Kari stole my virginity at the age of twelve. Dinner used to be served nightly at the main building for all kids and staff. One night after dinner, one of the teenage girls from the Heston House asked me to walk her back to her building. She was a couple of years older than me. Suddenly, she took a detour to a building on the grounds that had been a chicken coop and was now used for storage. She took me in, closed the door, and began kissing me. I had kissed a few girls already, but not like I was being kissed now, with mouths open and tongues touching. I liked it! Soon, Kari was unbuttoning her blouse. Kari wasn't very pretty but had a very mature body for a young teenage girl, and she was more than willing to share it with me. She guided my hands and fingers to the right places and finally consummated our chance meeting. The whole episode was a bit scary at first for a twelve-year-old boy but turned out very satisfying. This was one of those incidents that being raised in a home with other teenagers had its rewards. There were many times that boys and girls visited one another's rooms during the night, almost always undetected by houseparents. It is worthy to note that the girls initiated most of these sexual escapades. I'm not sure if this was because girls matured quicker than boys, because the girls were more daring, or because so many of the girls had had previous sexual experiences, usually at the hands of a parent, relative, or some other male who was in an authority position.

Jeremy Whiston came to the home about the same time I did and was a resident there until he graduated from high school. Jeremy was three years older than me. Jeremy eventually became my brother-in-law. He married my sister, Michelle. They had two great kids. They were married for twenty-three years, divorced, but have remained good friends. Jeremy was always a bit of a bully. He had a temper. Jeremy always worked very hard, both as a teenager and as a young man. He was very devoted to my sister. He came from a good-sized family, but none of the other children ever came to the home. Jeremy seemed to have more contact with his family than most of the kids. There were at least two instances when I can remember Jeremy getting into physical scuffles with male houseparents. Neither of these turned out badly but could have.

Dirk and Charlotte Darvin were brother and sister. Dirk was about four years older than me, and Charlotte was two years older. Dirk and Charlotte were like us kids—they spent nearly their entire lives as children at the Burnside Children's Home. It was Dirk, who came up with the idea of calling kids he was mad at a cootie. Dirk had a real bad stuttering problem but was a good guy. Charlotte was more intelligent than most of the kids and went on to get a college degree. I had occasion to see Dirk and Charlotte a couple of years ago. Charlotte is a college professor at Northern Illinois University, and Dirk is retired.

One thing I find quite surprising—no one has attempted a reunion of us kids. This is a project I would like to attempt someday. Maybe this would be easier after this story is published. I am also surprised that more kids have not kept in touch with each other or that they haven't attempted to do more in this regard by contacting local people. There must be an underlying reason for this. I suspect that a lot of the kids are either ashamed that they lived in a children's home in the first place, or their experience was negative enough that they regret it and want to simply forget it. Perhaps these adults are just trying to manage their day-to-day lives.

A few years ago, I wrote an article for our newsletter at a bank where I worked. The story was about my Christmas gift from the Rooks, about the *band* shirts. Several weeks later, one of my coworkers told me that her mother had read the story and then relayed to Barb that she too had grown up at the Burnside Children's Home. Barb was about forty years old, and this was the first time she had ever heard this. Her mom said she never said anything because she was ashamed. I felt badly for this lady and others like her. I also feel so fortunate that my experience was positive, and I can talk freely about it. I also am glad that my short article prompted someone to deal with her own situation. I hope that most kids feel differently than Barb's mom and are able to share their experiences with others in a positive way, especially with their own children. Hopefully, past residents of the home will get a chance to read my book and will gain something from it.

HALLOWEEN

Halloween is an exciting time for any kid. You can imagine the excitement created by twenty or thirty kids gearing up for the event. We didn't have money to buy costumes, so we made our own out of whatever we could beg, borrow, or steal. Parties were usually held at school the same day, so we were geared up. The excitement started as soon as school was out and we could hardly wait for it to get dark. You need to remember that trick or treating used to be done at night, in the neighborhoods. Today, a lot of the fun is taken out of the event because trick or treating is done in business districts, during daylight hours or in malls. When darkness fell, we were off like racehorses from the gate. We went out trick or treating in groups—all picking blocks and areas where we felt the most riches would be found. Along the way, we would encounter each other and compare notes. Being kids, we naturally played some tricks. We knocked over our share of pumpkins and decorations, threw vegetables at houses, and tried to scare the younger kids. Nothing serious, just fun kid stuff. The best part of the night, however, was going back to the home with all the candy. We would dump our respective treasure on our individual beds and proceed to trade with each other. By bedtime, we all had had our favorite treats and went to bed, no doubt, with bellyaches. Whether it was Halloween, Valentine's Day, or whatever holiday, the home always made sure that we were able to participate in the festivities, as long as we did not dance.

HOUSEPARENTS

It seems when I first came to the home we had a lot of young, single women as houseparents. Over the years, more married couples were hired. I'm sure this was an attempt to try to create more of a family environment. The job must have had some appeal. The pay was low, but three meals a day, laundry service, medical care, and a furnished apartment were provided. This had to have appeal for young couples finishing college or changing careers. Since the people who worked there were all from the church, I am sure they received a lot of personal gratification for the Christian work they were doing.

It had to be difficult for the children of houseparents. All of a sudden, they were living in a children's home too. They had to abide by a lot of the same rules and regulations as the rest of us. Sometimes the kids at the home resented the children of houseparents because they didn't have to adhere exactly to our schedules and rules. Naturally, if one of the kids was punished by a houseparent, the other kids ostracized their children. I'm sure one of the reasons for houseparent turnover had to do with the stress of raising their own children in that environment. I don't remember there ever being any serious problems or relationships between home kids and the houseparent's children.

Looking back, I realize that a job as houseparent at the home was a pretty good place to find a husband. I remember at least five ladies who worked as houseparents and married local men from the church.

Most houseparents were there for a fairly short time. It seemed they were using the job as an interim step. Most were finishing up degrees and found this a good way to have a schedule that allowed the flexibility needed. I'm sure they didn't expect the emotional turmoil they encountered. They had to have made some attachments with certain children. I don't care who you are, but it's not possible to work with a group of children and not find ones who you like and dislike.

There seemed to be a lot of ministers who worked at the home over the years. They mainly worked as business managers or assistants to the executive director. They never stayed long. Again, it was as if they were using this job in a temporary situation while furthering their education or looking for other employment. I usually was able to make friends with most of the adults who worked at the home. I found them to have genuine interest in the kids. I remember one retired minister, Judd Torrance. His wife was Trudy. They had a son, Samuel, and a daughter whose name I don't recall. I got along with them very well. They rented a house in Winterlake, a community just seven miles east of Burnside. They invited me to their home for dinner several times. I liked them and had kind of a crush on Mrs. Torrance. I thought at one time they might ask me to live with them, but that never happened. They didn't stay at the home long. I'm pretty sure they later divorced.

I found it interesting that many times houseparents or employees of the Burnside Homes came in family groups. The parents would be employed at the manor, and the children would be employed at the Children's Home. I can think of at least three examples of this happening. I'm pretty sure these families had some sort of financial problems or there were health problems involved. They were all good people, but sometimes I got the impression that the staff at the Burnside Homes had lives not that different than what was experienced by some of us kids in our real homes. You just don't realize things like that as a child growing up; your outlook is totally different.

Looking back, maybe all the short-term houseparents weren't so bad. It probably prevented burnout, which is a common cause for abuse in that field and it probably prevented a lot of long-term relationships from developing between children and houseparents that would eventually lead to further heartache.

I probably had forty different houseparents or sets of houseparents over the years at the home. Some I became attached to; others I did not care very much for. There was one set of houseparents that had a more profound effect on my life than any others. Their influences on my life were both positive and negative, and I will explain that below.

Don and Joan Major

Mr. and Mrs. Major arrived at the Heston House, where the teens lived, on a Saturday afternoon. They had a Volkswagen Beetle car. These cars were just becoming popular in America at the time, but I had never actually been inside one. A separate truck had brought their belongings. As with all houseparents, the Majors stayed in the small efficiency apartment that was furnished on the first floor. It was nice, but small, with a kitchen, private bath, bedroom, and living room. The living room was usually used by the kids as well as a place for dates or to visit relatives. A couple of us teenage boys, as usual, helped move in the furniture and their belongings. Mr. Major seemed like a very down to earth kind of guy. He worked right alongside us and even offered to pay us for helping. His wife was very nice and offered us some lemonade and cookies after we were done working. Don offered us coffee, which I took. Coffee was one of the things Don and I would always have in common. I still drink a lot of strong, black coffee.

Don and Joan came from Ohio. Don had recently retired from the United States Army. I think Joan had done some kind of practical nursing back in Ohio. Don always had good stories to tell about his travels and experiences in the army. Some of the stories were about drinking and doing the kinds of things men do while in the service and unsupervised. We boys were surprised, but pleased, that he shared these things with us. I didn't think that Joan approved. Don had a flat top haircut and was very military in his bearing. His posture was straight, his clothes were very neatly pressed, his shoes were shined, and he spoke in a commanding voice. While in the army, he had been a heavy smoker and drinker and had a lot of experiences that most of our previous houseparents had not. I thought it was good that us teenage boys might be able to hear something about real life rather than just stories about church-related activities. He even occasionally told an off-colored story to us. I don't think that Don was as religious as Joan. He made some friends outside the home that were not members of our church, and he seemed to like to get away from it all with them once in a while. As an adult, I can understand that. While houseparents, Don pretty much ran the house like a military. He required strict scheduling, clean quarters, attention to time and detail, and did not tolerate insolence or anyone not following orders. Don and Joan's biggest failure as houseparents was that they played favorites and were very obvious about it. This naturally caused a lot of resentment among the other teens.

As it turned out, I was one of the favorites. From day one, I hit it off with the Majors. After helping them move, we got a little chance to know each other. I think Don liked that fact that I fit in well with his military style. I liked and adhered well to a schedule. I dressed well and kept myself very clean. On Sunday evening, Don and Joan walked to church with me and my roommate, and we sat with them. Joan was very pleased that I enjoyed singing. The three of us really hit it off from the start.

I'm not sure if it was that Don needed to get away from it all a lot or if he just enjoyed driving his beetle, but he was always driving kids everywhere—to work, school activities, dates, or just to visit friends. I don't remember any other houseparent being willing to do that. Their attitude was always, "You can walk if you want to go." I remember a lot of mornings I would wake early, and Don and I would go for a morning drive. He would buy donuts and coffee, and we just rode somewhere. I enjoyed this time very much. Don gave me some new insights into my world. I felt that I might have a father figure that I could count on for help and counseling. He was interested in my school activities. He encouraged me to have friends outside the home. He was the one who got me to start taking voice lessons. He taught me how to drive. After Don and Joan were no longer houseparents, their home was always open to me. I could always go there to visit or even spend the night. After graduating from high school and going to college, I always had a room wherever they lived.

I didn't realize it at the time or did not want to acknowledge it, but Don very definitely had an unhealthy interest in teenage boys. I can assure you that he never made any advances toward me, but he did occasionally put his hand on my knee while driving, and he once in a while kissed me on the forehead. I think he knew it made me feel uncomfortable. I'm not sure exactly what his relationship was with other boys at the time. He always had one or two favorites that he spent a lot of time with and gave them a lot of extra attention. If one boy would move away, he would immediately have another friend. He would even befriend boys from the community and have them over to the home. I don't think management at the home cared much for that. Knowing a lot more about life today than I did then, I am pretty sure that Don probably had some inappropriate times with some of these boys. He always seemed to pick out easy prey. He liked to befriend boys who had troublesome homes and lives, especially ones whose fathers were not in their lives. I am not sure, but I think that this may have had something to do with the Majors being relieved of their houseparent duties, but maybe not, since they were still employed at the home for several years in different capacities. Some of the other kids, especially the girls, said Don was gay and even made insinuations about him and me. This was very hurtful. Even though I was not close to all of the kids at the home, I was always sticking up for them and even getting into fights with other kids to support them, so this attitude really hurt. I realize now that the feelings they had were directed more at Don than they were at me. His actions probably seemed more overt since he and Joan did not have an affectionate relationship. I don't think I ever saw them kiss, hold hands, or show any physical affection to one another. Additionally, Joan was also close to some of the girls and had lady friends from the church who she would walk about the grounds with their arms around each other's waists. She too had teenage girls that were her favorites. I would have thought these actions would have been red flags to other people at the home, and maybe they were, but the Majors were houseparents for two to three years.

While the Majors were my houseparents, I went through a period of being a quitter. I would join something and then would quit. I quit freshman football, basketball—even after the coach had asked me to join the team— and track. I didn't seem to want to spend the time practicing or do the hard work that was required. This was very unlike me. One Sunday night after church services, Walter Trinton, a former houseparent at the home and now a teacher at Burnside High School, said he would like to talk to me. Mr. Trinton gave me a real fatherly talk. He told me that teachers at school and even some of my friends were really disappointed in me lately, especially because of me quitting everything. He said that he thought the reason I was doing this was because I wanted to join these activities, but Don Major did not want me to. Mr. Trinton felt that Don wanted me to spend time with him. I realized that Mr. Trinton was right. It helped to clarify to me why I was changing behaviors suddenly and so drastically. This was during baseball season that Mr. Trinton and I had this talk. I stuck with teener league that year and kept pretty busy that summer working my part-time jobs. I worked at putting some distance between Don and me. I think he knew I was a pretty healthy, normal young man, and I was not interested in anything inappropriate. Don and I always remained good friends. I had a lot of respect for him as a man, and he gave me a lot of good advice while he was my houseparent.

I was a little surprised that Walt Trinton had that talk with me. He and his wife were houseparents for several years at the home but were mine for just a short while. The Trintons always liked my sister, Michelle, very much, but I never thought they liked me. There was always something missing. My sister, Colleen, shortly before leaving the home, didn't get along with them very well either. In fact, she hit Mr. Trinton in the lip and left a scar. It was shortly after that incident that she went to live with the Wilbrandts in Michigan. Once, during the short time he was my houseparent, I had punched a boy in the mouth and knocked out his two front teeth. I probably did him a favor since he had very bad buck teeth. Anyway, Mr. Trinton and I were at the top of the stairs going to the boy's dorm, and he told me, "Andy, you have to learn to control your temper." He then proceeded to grab me by the back of the neck and pushed me down the stairs. I landed on the landing halfway down the stairs. I was unhurt, but I am not sure I got the message he was sending very clearly. While an adult, I became much more friendly with Mr. Trinton. He shopped in my store occasionally and supported me when I ran for city council. Mr. Trinton died a few years ago. I was sad. I actually had good feelings about him. A couple of years ago, my sister, Michelle, invited Mrs. Trinton and two of her children to her house. I went as well. We had a nice visit, and I was happy to see that their children were doing well and had nice families.

TOLERANCE

I'm afraid the home didn't do a very good job of teaching the children about tolerance. In the eleven years I lived there, there was not even one African American child, no one of Asian descent and maybe one or two Latino children. In all fairness though, I have to admit that in the 1950s and early 1960s, there were not many people of color in Burnside, Illinois, which is where most of the kids came from. I'm not sure any Catholic children were there; and certainly there were no children of lesser known faiths such as Hindu, Muslim, or even Jewish. I'm sure part of this was because the home was a fundamentalist-church-run operation, but there were lots of kids there who came through the court system and not from church channels.

The church taught us from the Bible that we are all born equal and to "love thy neighbor," but in practice, we were not taught by example to be tolerant of other races and religions. Any other religions just were not tolerated. It took years for me to become convinced that Catholicism was not some sort of cult to be avoided. By today's standards, I would have to say that people at the home and church were pretty right wing in their thinking. The community itself was very white, conservative, and intolerant in its thinking. For many years, Burnside had only one black family. Ernie Bates worked at the City of Burnside water department. His daughter, Rhoda, was in my class in school. Perhaps this was an area that the home could have expended more energy on rather than so much concentration on Bible study and music. Most of the people I run into who were residents of the home seem to be quite narrow minded in their thinking, and I think that may be a result of our upbringing at the home.

THE JOB MARKET

My first job, at age nine, was a paperboy. I delivered the *Burnside Daily Sentinel*, the local daily paper. I had a large route, seventy-two papers, that was in the vicinity of the home. The cost was thirty cents per week for customers. I got to keep seven cents plus tips. I learned that each customer wanted the paper delivered in a different manner. Some wanted the paper in the mailbox, some inside the front door, and some on the doorstep. I walked my route because I could give much better service than riding a bike. As a paperboy, I learned about customer service. I've always had great customer service skills, and I attribute some of that to what I learned delivering newspapers. I also learned about collections. It was each boy's responsibility to make sure he got paid. I learned to follow up and be persistent in my collection efforts. This no doubt aided me in the future as a collection officer in a bank for eight years. I enjoyed my customers and for many years enjoyed seeing these people about town even as an adult. I also learned at a young age the importance of showing up for work every day. I found that success came from hard work, diligence, and treating people right. I enjoyed my paper route and took it very seriously. I won several contests for having the least complaints and a couple for signing up the most new subscriptions. It is really interesting to look back and see how some management principles used in business today really were no different than with a nine-year-old paper boy doing his route. I recall one contest I won where the prize was a trip to a Chicago Blackhawks hockey game. I won the contest but never collected. The circulation manager for the paper suddenly left town. Apparently, he had absconded with some company funds as well as the tickets. I don't remember ever being compensated for winning the contest. Oh, well, another lesson in the workplace.

My next job was washing dishes at the Old People's Home. This was tedious and hard work. I had to run the big dishwasher for about two hours a night seven days a week. The job paid fifty cents per hour. I got along well with the old people. I used to sing while I washed the dishes, and the old people seemed to like that. Maybe that was because they couldn't hear very well.

In the seventh grade, I got a job mowing a lawn for an older couple that lived down the street from Reverend Keating. The Greists were good people. They were demanding but taught me how to take care of a yard. They had no children and were very fussy about things. Mr. Greist owned a small metal-treating business in town, B & J Metal Products. When I turned sixteen, he let me work at the factory doing clean-up work and odd jobs. I enjoyed the camaraderie with the guys at the shop; but the work was hard, dirty, and boring. It probably helped me to decide to go to college. The Greists were also good to me. Mr. Greist even offered to help me with college if I would stay working at the shop. I was too young and didn't really understand what an opportunity I was being given. I guess I was also somewhat confused. The Greists really liked me and wanted to help me, but I was looking for a home, which did not fit into their plans. I remained friends with the Greists for many years. They shopped in my store, made a donation to my mayoral campaign, and even became a banking customer of mine years later. I often wondered how differently my life would have turned out if I had developed that relationship further. However, there was not that warm bond that would be necessary for a personal relationship. I think we both knew that.

Throughout junior high and high school, people were always giving me part-time or one-time jobs. I mowed lawns, babysat, washed windows, cleaned houses, washed cars, and even helped cut down trees. I liked being around adults, and I liked having money in my pocket. I liked the freedom I was afforded by being away from the home. Sometimes it meant a great deal to just have a half hour that I didn't have to account for. I was able to forge some friendships with other young people I met and also with adults who were not associated with the home. I was exposed to more aspects of life than the home and church showed me, and I saw how regular people lived their lives. I met a few girls that I dated while working. Unfortunately, having all those jobs did little to prepare me for college, except for saving money. When I graduated from high school in June of 1967, I had saved up $2,000 for college. That was a lot of money back then saved from washing dishes, stocking shelves, and cleaning toilets. One year later, the money was gone, and I had to transfer from Brownsville College to the local community junior college.

During high school, I had a couple of jobs that I really enjoyed and that were not quite so mundane in nature. The first was at the F.W. Woolworth store, located on the square in Burnside. My first duty there was to scrape away all the gum that was stuck under the lunch counter. Yuck! I guess Mr. Mann, the manager, wanted to see if I had the guts to work hard. I showed him. After that I enjoyed the various duties, like stocking shelves, checking in merchandise and helping customers find merchandise. People from the home and the church and kids from school would come in the store and see me working. I felt kind of important and liked that feeling. I met a lot of people there and made some long-term friends. Working there kind of got retail in my blood I think. I was to work retail in one fashion or another for the next twenty years.

I worked for about a year at a local food chain. I stopped by one evening on a whim. Some of my friends worked there, and I knew they had very flexible hours. I heard the pay was good, so I thought I might be able to fit some additional hours into my work schedule. Mr. Rock hired me on the spot. Years later, as an adult, he told me that he didn't really need any new help at the time he hired me, but he hired me because he liked my smile. Earnest Rock and I were friends until the day he died many years later. I enjoyed working at the food store. The pay was good, the work was fairly enjoyable, not too difficult, and I was able to associate with my friends. It was at this time that I started enjoying times with my friends more. We would go out after work and try to pick up girls or just go out for a hamburger. I enjoyed the social aspect of this as much as the work.

I was fortunate enough to land a job at Whipple's Drug Store in the square in town. Can you believe it? The owner of the drugstore was Mr. Whipple, just like in the Charmin toilet paper advertisement on television. This was a Walgreen's pharmacy. I delivered prescriptions, cleaned the floors and bathroom, washed windows, stocked shelves, and even got to handle the cash register on occasion. My first night on the job the weather was cold and snowy. I made a delivery in Mr. Whipple's 1957 Chevrolet. Having driven very little, I had put the emergency brake on and it froze. Mr. Whipple wasn't very pleased, but we got through it. Mr. Whipple was always cranky but was pretty good to me. I enjoyed the work and also being in the public eye. Mr. Whipple had bad body odor, which was accentuated by the nylon smocks he wore. One evening, a lady came in and wanted to buy some deodorant. Mr. Whipple was helping her. He pointed out a bottle on the shelf and said, "This is the one I use." I said to my coworker, Don, "I think I would buy the one next to it." Mr. Whipple apparently heard my remark and gave me a dirty look, but I never heard more about it. Although Mr. Whipple was gruff, it was a nice place to work.

While working these other jobs, I filled in time with a job at the Butternut Bakery Outlet located in Burnside. I cleaned the bathrooms, mopped floors, and helped load and unload the bakery trucks. Yes, I was allowed to help myself to the tasty treats. This was hard work, but what I really liked about the job was my boss, Ray Amaan. Ray was a good-hearted, hot-headed guy who really took a liking to me. He invited me to go to coffee with the guys, which I really liked. He invited me to his house for dinner and even let me borrow his black 1962 Buick Skylark convertible for dates a couple of times. I became quite close to Ray and his wife, LaVerne. There was even some discussion about me possibly living with them, but that never materialized. I'm sure I am the one brought up the idea. I always felt that Ray was the kind of man I would have liked as a father at that stage of my life. He was fun, but firm, and always gave good advice. Ray and I remained friends as adults. He shopped in my store, and I would occasionally run into them around town. Ray and his wife retired and moved to Arkansas, and I never saw them again.

I was very mature for my age. I was big for my age, looked several years older than I actually was, and, for some reason, preferred to spend more time with adults than with people my own age. Maybe that's because of the amount of time I spent in the hospital as a child. Maybe it is because I didn't interact well with other kids because of my problem with uncontrollable bed and pants wetting. Whatever the reason, this facet of my personality has been a mixed blessing for me. While my association with adults allowed me extra privileges and let me get to know a lot of people, it hampered my childhood development. I took life much too seriously. I didn't take part in children's games, as I should have. I have never read a whole comic book in my life, but I did read most of the Bible. I didn't like cartoons very much, preferring westerns and cop shows. While other kids were playing marbles, I was playing chess. As a child, I didn't learn the value of playtime. I felt it was for kids. As an adult, unfortunately, I have tended to act the same way. Time off and vacations have never been important to me. As a result, I have probably exposed myself to a lot more stress than necessary. Furthermore, I, in turn, have probably caused extra stress for others.

I learned early on at the home that in order to survive and, hopefully, do better than merely survive, I had to interact with the adults. I learned that I could actually manipulate them sometimes. I found that if I didn't cause problems for them, they would reward me by letting me bend the rules. This certainly made my life easier.

THE COLLEGE EXPERIENCE

Teachers at school and people at the home were always saying that I should go to college. I think they were thinking in more of a general sense. I think they meant, "You don't want to work in a factory all your life," rather than them providing any real help and direction to me. During my junior and senior years in high school, I did begin to give college more thought, although I was still expending most of my energy on my jobs instead of school work. I took the SAT test and applied to colleges. I filled out applications for financial aid and small grants and scholarships, any place that I heard there might be money available, but had no luck. I was accepted at Brownsville College, Roosevelt University, Eastern and Northern Illinois Universities. I actually accepted at Northern Illinois University in DeKalb, Illinois. I figured I could drive there to classes two or three days a week and then keep some of my part-time jobs. I drove there one day to register. When I got there, I was intimidated. I didn't realize how far a drive it was. I got lost on campus the first day, had no idea where I was going, and just felt lost. I was afraid that was how college was going to be. After a couple of hours of wandering and becoming frustrated, I got in my car and drove back to Burnside, giving up on the idea of attending college at a state university. A couple of weeks later, I took the train to downtown Chicago and visited Roosevelt University. Again, I thought I could commute and keep working. I was not prepared for Roosevelt. Everyone there, teachers and students alike, looked like hippies—not my style. I took the train back to Burnside and decided to look at another plan.

This was a point in my life where I really needed parents. I needed adults that really cared about my welfare that could help me sort out this college thing. Adults around the home tried, but they all wanted me to go to Brownsville because it was associated with the church. That was all well and good, but there was very little financial help available, and Brownsville cost a lot more than the state schools. I was a little surprised that there was

113

not more financial help for someone who had grown up in the Burnside Homes, which was an arm of the same organization—the church. Plus, I have to admit, I was being a little rebellious. I was trying to get out from under the thumb of the home and the church. Well, when it came right down to it, I decided to go to Brownsville. The college did have a good reputation. There were a few people from the church that I knew there, and probably most importantly, I felt safe going there.

The night before I left for college, my Aunt Lil came to visit me. She brought me an iron and a dictionary. I had the dictionary for probably thirty years. Bless Aunt Lil. She was always practical and looking out for me.

Bob and Joan Major, former houseparents, drove me to Brownsville, Illinois. Actually, Bob let me do a lot of the driving, which I enjoyed. Brownsville was a small Midwestern town, not a lot unlike Burnside. In fact, it even had a square downtown just like my hometown. Brownsville was located forty miles northeast of St. Louis, in Bond County. Not surprisingly, Brownsville was dry, not serving any alcohol. That wasn't a problem for me as I really had not started drinking at this point, but it certainly fit into the pattern I was used to. This was 1967. This was also the first year that students from Brownsville College were allowed to go to movies at the local theater. I was told by upper classmen that Dean Kemp used to sit in a tree across the street from the downtown theater and watch for college students sneaking into the show. Female students were not allowed to wear pants or slacks before 6:00 p.m. Naturally, smoking and dancing were strictly forbidden.

The college itself was located right in the middle of the town, occupying approximately four square blocks. The college had 1,200 students at the time. Being a Christian school, there were almost no problems caused by the college students. In fact, the local kids referred to us students as "BC queers." Most of the students just put up with that, but one night me and two other guys had enough. We were coming out of the theater, and two young guys sitting in a car yelled, "Hey, BC queers." We walked over to the car, pulled one of them out of the car, and punched him out really good. His big mouth buddy didn't even get out of the car to help him. They took off, the one guy with a bleeding face. I hope the story got around that not all the guys at the college were queers.

The first day of school should have been a clue. There was a minor earthquake, a tremor actually. Was the college being warned that I was coming? I got the key to my room and it took three tries to get the correct key. I'm afraid it never got much better at Brownsville. Even though I had grown up in a very similar environment all those years, I guess I was ready for a change. Many of the students there came from very sheltered homes and were behind in social development. If you swore, someone would report you to the dean, and you had to go before a student tribunal and get fined. Most of the girls had little experience with dating and all were scared to death of getting pregnant. Like most college students, money was short, and the activities we were allowed to do were limited, so we mostly dated by attending school functions with members of the opposite sex. There was a cemetery across the road from the girl's dorm where a lot of necking and petting went on after dark, but that's about as exciting as it got.

My first roommate, Steve, had to move back home after about a month. He was homesick and didn't care for dorm life. He was a nice guy and a really good basketball player. His dad was superintendent of schools for a small school district not too far way, so Steve moved back home and commuted. My second semester roommate, Larry, was a really good guy. He was from the next town east. Larry and I got along well and became friends. He became a nurse and eventually a prison warden in a local prison.

The teachers at Brownsville were good and really cared about educating the students. They were dedicated and always gave of their time. Classes were tough. This was a lot different than high school. Most students here were serious about their education and knew what field of study they were interested in and what they wanted to accomplish in their lives. I was not at that point. I found every day to be a challenge. I made a few friends, but most of them were like me. They were the ones who did not fit in as well. I was working part-time at the college, cleaning the dorm next door. That took time and helped with the money situation but also prevented me from having much time for fun.

The highlight of my year at Brownsville was being selected to the A Capella Choir. This was a prestigious choral group that the college sponsored. The choir traveled for the college regularly, and each year went on a tour over the Easter break. The year I was there, we traveled out West. We gave a concert in Phoenix, Arizona on Easter Sunday at an outside service that was very well attended, I remember. We traveled by bus to Arizona, Oklahoma, Kansas, and Missouri. We stayed in homes of congregation members from the local churches while we traveled. That was nice. Choir tour was fun, a lot of work, and a great experience for me.

The choir held practice three days a week at school. We performed every Sunday service and for the chapel service daily. The choir was a real commitment, but I was serious about music at the time, and the people at the home and church in Burnside were impressed that I was chosen in my freshman year. The only difficulty I had with choir was that I never learned to read music very well. We did some very challenging music, and there were a lot of talented kinds in the choir, so I had to work hard to keep up.

I lasted my freshman year, got passing grades, but was never happy at Brownsville, probably because it was too much like the Children's Home. I left after one year, broke and frustrated. My $2,000 was gone. I had worked hard in a lot of ways that year and felt like it was all wasted time. I headed back to Burnside on the Illinois Central Railroad. I think about riding that train every time I hear the Arlo Guthrie song, "City of New Orleans" about that particular train. The train was one way to get from Greenvile to Burnside. Another way was to get rides from other kids going back and forth to the Chicago area, which happened pretty regularly. The other alternative was hitchhiking. Looking back, I can't believe I hitchhiked, but times were different then and people were more trusting. I remember one time I had hitched rides up to Chicago to see a girl I liked. We had a nice weekend together, and then I had to hitchhike back. I caught a good ride on the south side of Chicago that took me all the way to Bloomington. I got a couple more rides that got me to Litchfield, Illinois, about thirty miles from Brownsville. Then I got caught in an awful rainstorm. I had no umbrella. I walked several miles then found a bridge under a highway that I was able to stand in to keep dry. Eventually, a car with kids returning to Brownsville came by, saw me, and gave me a ride. That day was quite an experience.

I worked that summer at a local men's store where I worked the previous summer. I had also worked there on breaks from school. The owner was nice about that. Anytime I came home for the weekend, I could just show up and work for the day or days I was home. I really enjoyed meeting the public and dressing up every day. I was renting a room from the Majors at the time, and they encouraged me to stay in college. It was a difficult decision. Working full-time put money in my pocket, gave me some time to have some fun for a change, and I didn't have any homework to do. However, I realized that I should go to college. A local community junior college was opening in its first year in the fall of 1968 in a neighboring town, which was a good opportunity for me. By juggling schedules, I was able to work pretty much full-time at the men's store, take a full load at the college, and pay for school without incurring more debt.

The year at junior college as we referred to it, went well. I actually made the Dean's List for the first time in my life. I had acquired some good study habits at Brownsville, which paid off. I made some new friends and acquaintances, sang in the school choir, and was even pegged for the lead role in *Guys and Dolls*, but then funding for the production was pulled, and it never happened. There were quite a few older adults in the classes at MCC. I remember thinking to myself, "Boy, I don't want to be going to college when I am forty years old." I received my associate's degree at the end of the year. I found that I really enjoyed working more than I enjoyed college and decided not to look into attending school anywhere for my junior year. In retrospect, this was a mistake. Ten years later, I took night courses at the National College of Education in Evanston, Illinois to receive my bachelor's degree. It was nice to have the degree, but the education was very general. I really did not learn a trade or specific discipline. This has not been helpful to my career, and the older I get I find that not finishing college right away was one of the most unwise decisions of my life.

In May of my junior year of high school, the assistant principal called me to his office. This was not a totally unusual event. He said the Post Office was initiating a program to hire high school seniors to work part-time in an effort to attract more employees. He knew I needed the money and liked to work. He recommended me for the job. It was a great job. The pay was $3.57 an hour. That was a huge amount of money for a high school kid in 1966. The downside was that I had to work Monday through Friday from 5:30 to 7:30 a.m. I also worked eight hours on Saturday and special occasions. I worked with a lot of nice people. I filled mail sacks, delivered mail, and put mail in boxes that people rented. I worked very hard. I didn't want to lose that job. One early morning, I was stuffing mail into the large, dirty sacks. I was sweating because it was hot. The assistant postmaster, Bruce Steinke, came over to me and said, "Andy, slow down. Nobody sweats at the Post Office." In February of 1967, the Chicago area was hit with a horrendous snow storm. We got twenty-four inches of snow. Naturally, schools were closed. I was happy because they I could spend the day working. However, three mail carriers called in sick that day, and I had to deliver a lot of mail in that snow to help out. There were two other funny things that I remember. The first was that I was told the program would be for one year. After the year ended, I moved on to another job. The postmaster's daughter was a classmate of mine. She met me on the street one day and questioned why I had quit. No one bothered to tell me I could stay on. I could be retired now. Secondly, I received a check for $400 about a month after I quit. I didn't know what it was for. Being an honest, dumb kid, I was afraid to cash it so I inquired as to why I received it. I was told it was unused sick pay and vacation pay. Wow! I had never heard of such a thing as benefits before. This was another time when some parental guidance would have come in handy. Someone should have told me that I could stay on at the post office, and it would have been good if someone could have explained the good benefits associated with working for the government. I can't really fault the home. They had fifty kids to worry about, not just me. I'm sure they were just happy that I was employed and not causing any problems.

Maybe because my dad farmed, I thought I wanted to work on a farm the summer between high school and college. A fellow I worked with at the post office knew a lot of farmers and said he would find me a job, which he did. It was a very nice farm, owned by Bornhoff Dairy of Berwyn, Illinois. It had a modern milking system and beautiful Harvistore silos. My primary responsibility was to milk approximately one hundred cows twice daily, at 4:30 a.m. and 4:30 p.m. This was in addition to the normal farm chores. I cleaned the barns, fed the animals, built a fence, and helped deliver a calf and lots of other varied tasks. I worked hard, got along with the boss and his wife, and enjoyed working in the fresh air. The pay was good too. However, I really wasn't a farmer at heart, and I wasn't at all mechanically adept. One day, I showed up for work, and the boss met me in the barn. The conversation went like this: "You know, Andy, you're a good kid. You're honest and hardworking, but you're really not a farmer."

I said, "You want me to quit?"

Bob (the boss) said, "Yeah."

I responded, "Good."

Bob and I parted company that day. No hard feelings. We remained friends ever since. Looking back, I wonder if that shouldn't be in a management book as the most honest and direct "exit interview" on record.

After the exit from the farm, I got into my 1959 Chevy and drove back to town. I remember crying in the car. Here I was, heading off to college in a few weeks, and I was out of a job. I went home, showered, put on my only suit, and headed downtown to prospect for a job. I parked in front of Beard & Stovall, the town's finest men's store. I walked into the store, encountered the owner and told him I was looking for a job. He asked when I could start and I said, "right now." I did just that.

That two-hour period was the longest period I have ever been unemployed since the age of thirteen. I didn't like the feeling of insecurity of not having a job. My work has always been extremely important to me. Most of my life until the age of forty-eight, I've always worked two jobs at a time.

A PERFECT GENTLEMAN

The restaurant was very nice. Well laid out, nice linen tablecloths, quality place settings, and the food was delicious. My client's secretary, Theresa, said to me, "Wow, you have such good manners." Manny, the client said, "Yes, I've always noticed that about Andy." From the first day at the home, we were always taught to have manners. I remember that table manners were a priority:

- Don't chew with your mouth open.
- Put the napkin on your lap.
- Always use the utensil furthest to your left.
- Take the food with your right hand and pass with the left. Few people know that one.
- Don't begin eating until everyone is seated.
- Don't take the last food from the dish.

Table manners weren't all:

- Always let the lady go first.
- Always open the door for a lady.
- Shake hands and make eye contact when you meet.
- Say "Please" and "Thank you" when appropriate.
- Respect your elders. Address them as Mr. or Mrs.
- Don't interrupt when others are speaking, especially adults.

These are just a few of the mantras we were taught. Institutional living has to have rules and parameters, but the people at the home went above and beyond to teach us manners and polite behavior. I can't recall the number of times in my life people have commented about my good manners.

When people learn that I was raised in a children's home, they are truly amazed. People have these preconceived notions that we lived the way Oliver Twist did in Charles Dickens' time. People constantly tell me or I hear them say to others, "Andy is such a perfect gentleman."

DRESS FOR SUCCESS

"Andy that shirt you have on is out of style. Get with it, man." Those words from Toby really stung. I was in seventh grade. I played first string on the football and basketball teams. I was popular. On this day, I was walking home from school with some friends. I don't know what brought Toby's comment about, but I made up my mind then and there that I would never have to hear another comment like that. I decided that I was always going to dress nice. I already cared about how I looked but was not getting any good direction about style, color, etc.

A lot of the clothes we got at the home were hand-me-downs or were donations from the Salvation Army, Whiston College, or from people in the community. We seldom got new clothes. Occasionally, we got some new clothing from the local Montgomery Wards store if we were in desperate need. That was a real treat. Each Christmas, clothing topped my Christmas list. When I started working, I bought myself new clothes. I would ask advice from my housemothers, sister, and other girls at the home as to how I looked and if colors went together. I learned to do my own ironing at the age of twelve and have ironed my own shirts all of my life. One of the things I liked about going to church was that we had to wear a suit, shirt, and tie. Most of the kids hated wearing ties, but I enjoyed it. I wear a tie every day for work and feel naked without one. I tell people, "I feel so comfortable in a tie I could wear one to mow the lawn."

Years later, when I owned my own clothing store, the father of the boy who insulted me about my clothes became a sometime customer of mine. The father was just like the son. He wanted to look good and be in style. Unfortunately, he couldn't afford to dress well. I often wanted to say something about his son's rude comments to me, but I always held my tongue. My own success was sweet enough revenge.

That day in the seventh grade when Toby made his comment, there was another boy with us. His name was Ernie. Ernie was probably the most popular boy in school throughout junior high and high school. Ernie was good looking, always well dressed, funny, and just a great guy to be around. Ernie's parents took a liking to me and Dennis, the other kid from the home with whom I played sports at school. After our final football game—we had won our conference, undefeated—Ernie's parents took all of us out for dinner at a fancy restaurant in neighboring town. It was called Haznows. The restaurant is still in the same location but has changed hands. It was the fanciest restaurant I had been to in my young life. I felt really special and we had a great time. I remember wanting to put catsup on my steak. They politely told me about steak sauce. Unfortunately, during basketball season, I got a hernia and had to have surgery. While in the hospital, Ernie's parents came to the hospital to visit. When I got home and was recovering, they stopped by one night and brought me two new shirts from the finest men's store in town. Man, was I pleased. I was very grateful to them for their caring and generosity. I was going to be right in style, just like Ernie. Years later, I came to know Ernie's parents as adults. It was really interesting. Ernie's dad didn't want to spend hardly any money on his own clothes and was actually known around town as being quite tight fisted. However, he and his wife were certainly generous and good to Dennis and me. I saw that Elmer and his wife sacrificed for their kids, and I was impressed. Toby's parents, on the other hand, were all about show and did not set a very good example for their children.

As I have grown older and matured, I still like to dress up and look nice. I always try to dress appropriately for any occasion. I care about how I look. People always comment that I dress well. I feel like I have come a long way since that embarrassing walk home from school in the seventh grade.

PANTRY RAID

It was four in the morning, and it was quiet and dark. The only light was the "Exit" sign above the dorm entry door. We didn't get up until 6:30 a.m., but Steve and I were hungry. We quietly got out of our beds and with great stealth made our way across the dorm and down the creaky stairway undetected. By now, we knew all of the creaky spots on each stair and could avoid the squeaky noise on each step by walking carefully and keeping our feet on the outsides of the stairs. Still in the dark, we crossed the floor of the recreation room and opened the door to the back porch. Then immediately to the right was the door to the kitchen. We went through both doors and entered the kitchen. At least we could see in there, as there was always a night light left on in the kitchen. Do you suppose they left it on for us? We quietly proceeded to the pantry—our goal. We had been making this trip to the pantry for several nights. We stocked up on cookies and candy and even took a stash back to our dorm. We were growing boys and needed our nourishment, right? We couldn't survive on just three meals a day.

We very carefully opened the pantry door. Hmmm . . . someone must have left the light on in there. We proceeded around the door and froze in terror. There sat Aunt Liz, the cook. She had her reading glasses on, sitting on a chair in the pantry. She laid her book in her lap and said, "Hi, boys. I have been waiting for you." We knew we were toast. A spanking was in order, or we were going to be grounded, maybe go without dessert for a week. Much to our surprise, and delight, she gave us a short rebuke, told us not to do it again, gave us our cookies and milk, and sent us back to bed. To our knowledge, our houseparents never found out about this incident, and we were not punished. We don't know if another boy squealed on us or if Aunt Liz just figured it out, but we didn't do it again. Aunt Liz had a son of her own, and she knew he got hungry during the night just like us.

THE ORIGINAL SCARY MOVIE

Annie Kugler, or her ghost, was moving about in the attic of the main building. You could hear her footsteps in the stillness of the night. Was she coming down the stairs? Sounds like it. We explained this to Richard, the latest new kid. We told him it was nothing to be scared of. Annie Kugler just liked to come down from her home in the attic to visit each new kid. She wanted to get to know who they were and what they looked like. She didn't always touch them; sometimes she just looked. She would always come while the boy or girl was asleep. Richard was about to wet his pants out of sheer panic. Of course, that was the idea. Every new kid had to go through the rite of initiation.

There was an old, abandoned, very scary-looking house on the home property. Some child at the home years ago had come up with the story that the ghost of Annie Kugler lived there. No one knew who Annie Kugler was, but it made a great story. The story goes that she abandoned the house after one of the kids burned it down, and she then moved to the attic of the main building. This made for a great story, especially since the attic was huge, dark, and musty smelling. The building was old, and you would hear so many strange noises during the night. You would always hear mice scurrying about, which added to the fears of every boy. Each new kid went through this rite of passage into the home. It was, in my mind, the original scary movie. It was bad enough that a little boy would be taken from his parents one day. Then that same night, he would be frightened half to death. It was a mean ordeal, but we all survived it.

FIRE DRILL

The day was sunny and warm in mid-May. I was lying in the Burnside Memorial Hospital, room 106. Four weeks earlier, my appendix had burst. I know when it happened because it felt like a hot knife was stuck into my stomach. I was sleeping on the top bunk in the boy's dorm and had to get off to go the bathroom. When I jumped down from the bed, it was when I had the awful pain. I had had emergency surgery, and the incision became infected, so here I was in the middle of the little league season lying in the hospital. B-o-r-i-n-g! My room was at the end of the wing and faced the local high school. About two in the afternoon, kids started pouring out of the school. It looked like they must be having a routine fire drill, except the kids looked more apprehensive. There seemed to be some real anxiety even on the teacher's faces. Maybe there was a real fire this time. That would be exciting! Maybe they would have to close the school for a while.

Two of the older kids from the home came over to my room window. They told me there was a bomb scare. Wow, that was cool. That was 1959. Who had ever even heard of such a thing? School was let out for the day while police searched the school for the bomb. No bomb was ever found. However, they did find out who had made the anonymous phone call. It was Scab" Burke, one of the kids from the home. Scab was unhappy with one of his teachers over a grade he had received on a test. He probably got the idea for the bomb scare from watching television. The scare created a lot of excitement in the local community. I recall that Scab was expelled from school for a while, most of us thought he was lucky for that, but I don't recall any further punishment from authorities. I'm not sure, but I think he may have been put on probation for a time. One of the other kids who was at the home at the time of the incident told me years later that Dave, or Scab, had gone on to a successful career, but I don't recall what it was. I don't think it was bomb making.

MUSIC AND ME

I am not sure exactly when I became interested in music, particularly vocal music and singing. I always enjoyed the music at church and loved the gospel harmony of male quartets that visited the church. I had always enjoyed singing as a child as well. I remember singing while I sang on the back porch while I lived with the Purtills. I bet the neighbors loved that. They must have gotten real tired of hearing "Home on the Range." While a youngster at the home, I used to swing a lot and would always sing. Fortunately for others, the swing set was not that close to the living quarters or neighbors. I vaguely remember singing in a chorus at school in the fifth grade and being told that I had a very good voice. I always liked to do what I felt I could do well, and I guess that is maybe when I decided to pursue music a little more seriously. In the sixth grade, I joined choir in junior high. I liked this very much. We had choir every day and performed at different school functions. In the seventh grade, Ms. Carter formed a male quartet, of which I was a member. I sang baritone. I loved that. I was mature for my age and my voice had developed quickly too. I was being asked to sing solos in church, school events, and for activities associated with the home. Sometime in eighth grade, I began taking private voice lessons, $2 per lesson. This was very helpful to me, and I enjoyed it immensely. Practicing my vocals was difficult, however. The other kids at the home did not enjoy hearing me, so I didn't practice as I should have. I tried taking piano lessons but had the same problem. I resent that I didn't continue with piano lessons, as I think this would have been a big help to my singing career. When I got to high school, I again joined the choir. I was given solo parts at concerts. People were asking me to sing at weddings, school functions, and even funerals by my junior year. I won the part of Enoch Snow in Carousel my sophomore year. That was a great experience. I remember that my dad actually came to one of the performances with my sister, Michelle. This was during his sober years. He seemed very proud of me, and I was happy about that. During my junior year, I was awarded a music scholarship to attend a Music Clinic at the University of Wisconsin at Madison for two weeks in the summer. This was a wonderful experience. It was stimulating and an intense two weeks of study. I learned quite a lot in that short time and was exposed to some serious musical study. However, I really enjoyed the freedom and college atmosphere. At night, we had some free time. We naturally paired off with members of the opposite sex and went on dates. We had curfew, but that was about the only rule. We lived in nice college dorms right on Lake Mendota and could walk to all of the classes. I didn't want to go back home. For the next few years, I did my occasional singing at weddings and funerals, but finally, I had to concentrate on my full-time job. The men's retail business required that I work Saturdays, and that interfered with most weddings. As the old saying goes, "Don't give up your day job." I did not.

VISITING THE ZOO

The bus pulled up in the gravel driveway in front of the main building of the home. It was midmorning on a bright summer day. A lot of well dressed, middle-aged people, mostly women, descended from the bus. I don't recall the name on the bus or where the people were from, but us kids knew their mission. They were there to *view* us, like we were animals in the zoo. People did this all the time. Sometimes they came in bus loads, like this particular day. It was an outing for them. Sometimes they came to Sunday church services and then came to the home for dinner afterward. For some reason, this exercise really bothered us on this particular day, maybe it was the heat, and a couple of us decided to have some fun. Several of us boys took off our caps, turned them upside down, and approached the ladies getting off the bus. We proceeded to *beg*. We told the ladies, "We're hungry. We haven't eaten in two days." Every one of the ladies dug into their purses and gave us some change. Flat out lie, of course, but we had some fun. The fun ended when Ms. Victory heard of our shenanigans and sent us all back to the dorm to be dealt with later. I'm sure the ladies on the bus knew that we did not go hungry. They just made themselves feel good by giving us a few coins.

The home received lots of visitors. Many people from other churches would simply stop by while driving through town. Because the home was a church charity, I guess they felt they had a right to just pop in and take a look. They were curious about how the home was run and what the kids looked like. I am sure these adults had discussions with their children afterward about how lucky they were to have a good home so they didn't have to be in a home like the kids they had just seen.

There were numerous *official* visitors as well. Inspectors from the state and county, social service agency workers, the health inspector, and fire marshal were some of those visitors. There was always someone there to make sure all was well. Anyone who visited always treated us nicely. We even got used to seeing some individuals on a regular basis. Whenever important people would be coming or if it was someone or some group that might make a nice donation to the home, we were required to wear our good clothes and were warned to be on our best behavior. The one begging incident being the exception, I generally looked forward to visitors. They were generally nice, sometimes generous, and it was always a new face. Although I liked routine and a schedule, it was always a pleasure to meet someone different with a different story to tell.

LET'S GO FOR A DRIVE

In the 1950s, Americans fell in love with the automobile. The Eisenhower administration had just completed the interstate highway system, the largest infrastructure project in history. Times were good. Everyone had a car. Gas was cheap. It became a way of life on Sunday afternoons for people to just say, "Let's take a ride" or "Let's go for a drive." Just get in that new car and drive it somewhere for a few hours.

Sunday afternoons was when almost all parents and relatives came to see us kids. As I grew older, I realized that this was because that's when people "went for a ride." Most of the people that came to visit me and my siblings all lived within about fifty miles of the home—an easy, pleasant Sunday afternoon drive. My Aunt Lil came from Wheaton. Shortly, Ida and Mida came from Elburn. The Newtons came from Auburn. Grandpa Zajak came from Chicago, a little longer commute.

Grandpa Zajak was my mom's real dad, and the first of my grandma Bolden's three husbands. He was now married to Helen. Grandpa Zajak worked at LaSalle Bank. Helen did not work. Whenever they drove to Burnside, they would bring us candy. The candy looked like it might have been something the bank gave away for free. They never sent presents at Christmas or birthdays. Whenever they came, they were always dressed very properly. I don't think Helen really enjoyed the visits very much. She never smiled. She actually kind of reminded me of that nasty lady from *101 Dalmatians*. I just got the impression that after church on an occasional Sunday, Grandpa Zajak would turn to Helen and say, "Let's take a ride."

MY SIBLINGS

It is now 2014. I am sixty-five years old now. I should give a short history of my life as an adult and tell what happened in the lives of my four sisters. Some of the details may be repetitious because they were part of another story.

My oldest sister, Karen, was seven years my senior. She went to work at a Typewriter factory in Burnside after high school. She ended up marrying her boss, Jim. Jim had never been married. Jim wore nothing but coveralls. Karen didn't like to dress up either. She was always kind of a tomboy. I used to joke that they looked like the people in Grant Wood's painting, **American Gothic**. Jim lived at home with his parents, on a farm in a neighboring community. Karen and Jim bought a two-flat in Burnside where they lived for years. After Jim's parents died, they moved back out to the family farm. That was the 1980s, and they still used an outhouse at the farm. For this reason, I seldom visited. Jim died of cancer at about sixty-five, and Karen was heartbroken. They really had a great marriage. She stayed on the farm. She liked taking care of the animals. She died of a heart attack at fifty-one, while riding the lawn mower.

Of all my four sisters, Karen and I were probably the most alike. Both of us had a good sense of humor, were hard workers, and were more gregarious than the other three girls. Like me, she loved dogs. I have fond memories of Karen. When she was a teenager, she used to come back to the main building to see me. She would take me down to the corner store and buy me pop and candy, or she would play catch with me, as she liked baseball just like me. School was hard for Karen. Like me, she had matured and grown up fast. She didn't have a lot of different friends, but she always had very loyal, long-time friends. She had a generous heart and a good spirit. After Jim and Karen married, they would invite the rest of the family to their house regularly. We always had fun and there was always a lot to eat. Jim was very good to Karen and to the rest of us. I am glad she found Jim. They had a happy life together.

I think our original home life probably was hardest on Karen, since she was the oldest. She had problems with men in her life prior to meeting Jim, and I think that was because she had been molested by a man who was supposedly a friend of the family. The man also had relations with my mother as well. In fact, I remember this man having sex with my sister, at a very young age, in a building on our farm, right in front of me. I was only five or six and didn't really understand at the time what was happening.

Karen had a temper that would explode occasionally. Like me, she would usually lose her temper when she was defending someone else because she felt they had been wronged. I feel like Karen was rewarded with Jim for the tough childhood she had. I am happy for her.

Colleen, the next oldest, was one and a half years younger than Karen. We always called her "Collie." Collie was the smartest of the five of us. She was always on the honor roll in school and got the most education of any of us. She lived at the home for about five years. It was a difficult adjustment for her. Luckily, she had our sister, Michelle. They were close in age and very close as sisters and friends. Collie's sharp and inquisitive mind got her into trouble. Plus, she was a fighter. It didn't take much for her to debate, argue or fight. Although she was at the home while I was, I really didn't have a lot of reaction with her. Because of the age difference, she was always in a different building from me. I remember hearing stories of her misbehavior. It was never anything serious and usually involved her roommate and friend, Johynn. She was just rebellious and really did not like living at the home.

Between Collie's freshman and sophomore years, a family from Michigan had contacted the home looking for a girl to move in with them. The family was large, with five kids of their own, and an adopted Korean girl. They lived on a farm. Collie was chosen to go live with them. I think she was chosen for several reasons. One reason was her behavior and another was her energy. She had boundless energy, and this would work out well there. Collie lived with the Wilbrandts through high school and while attending Harper Valley College, outside Ann Arbor, Michigan. Harper Valley College was affiliated with the Church, as were the Wilbrandts. As it turned out, the Wilbrandts request to take in a child was not completely magnanimous. Mrs. Wilbrandt was not that well, and she needed help with the family. Collie was used almost like a slave. This situation took an emotional toll on her later on in life.

Collie received a bachelor's degree from Harper Valley and a master's degree in psychology from Michigan State University. This is pretty amazing to me for all she went through while growing up. She worked in social work, did family and marriage counseling, and, finally, ended up working for Delco Remy in Indianapolis, where she headed up the employee assistance and counseling programs for the human resources department.

Collie had a hard time with relationships. She had married her college sweetheart. Mitchell was a very nice man. He treated her well and was a faithful husband. However, at this point in her life, I think she had her fill of the church, regimentation, and rules and wanted some freedom in her life. They divorced. For the rest of her life, she dated numerous men, lived with a couple of different ones, but never remarried. I really felt bad for her. Like the rest of us, she never had any good role models for marriage, and we were all subjected to the wrong kinds of relationships to observe.

I visited Collie at college one weekend with my sister, Michelle, and her boyfriend. That was a fun weekend. It was obvious that Collie was popular and well thought of. I was very proud of her. Collie had fixed me up with a date. She wasn't particularly attractive, but she was willing to put up with a sophomore in high school as a date for the evening. Even though I was a sophomore, I was big for my age and looked older. I probably fit in better physically as a college sophomore than a high school sophomore. I felt kind of cool dating a coed. On the way back home from the weekend, a terrible tornado went through the county where we lived and did some major devastation. The ride home through Crystal Lake, where the damage was most severe, kind of put a damper on the weekend.

I visited Collie at the Wilbrandts one summer for a two-week period. It was fun. They had a horse that I got to ride, they had a pond where we were able to swim, and there was a lot to do on the farm. I thought that Mr. Wilbrandt had kind of a mean streak. He enjoyed getting me to touch the electric fence. I could see that the parents relied heavily on Collie to do chores, housecleaning, and babysitting. Colleen endured all of this through high school and college.

Collie and Michelle always kept very close throughout their adult lives. They visited each other often and kept in constant touch. Occasionally, I would get to see Collie, but usually it was just the two sisters.

At the age of fifty, Collie committed suicide. According to Michelle and some of Collie's friends, she had just worn herself out. She had taken on too many problems of her clients and coworkers. She had not taken the time or put forth the effort to solve her own problems, which apparently were numerous. It was sad when we went to clean out her condo. She had done well financially. She had a good position in her career, but she was lonely. I guess Michelle was aware of Colleen's demons but had not shared it with me or anyone else.

One of Colleen's coworkers was kind enough to escort us to the funeral home and other places we needed to go the days we were in Indianapolis. She asked if we were going to have a visitation. We said we had not planned on it. She said, "Oh, you have to. So many people will want to attend." I thought she was exaggerating. She was not. The funeral home was packed with people for hours. Several people came up to me and said things like, "Your sister saved my life." "I wouldn't be here if it weren't for Colleen." I guess she was good at her job and really cared about people. Maybe she cared too much, and it wore her out emotionally. How sad. I wish that Collie and I had been closer over the years. Maybe I could have been of some help.

Linda was the youngest, a year and a half younger than myself. She had problems since early childhood. Being the youngest, I think our home life really had a bad effect on her emotionally. She was never strong physically or emotionally and was very dependent on others throughout her life. My Grandma Bolden, Mom's mother, always favored Linda and tried as much as she could to help her. Linda came to the home the same day as Karen and me. She was either in kindergarten or the first grade. School was hard for her. In the fourth or fifth grade, Linda was put in a foster home in Auburn, Illinois. She lived there through high school, although I remember that she was never very happy. The lady was very strict, even mean. I think that foster care was probably a good idea for Linda, but that particular home was not the answer. Linda never matured as she should have. She made it through high school and married a nice young man named Cole. Cole was kind to her and worked hard. They had two boys. Cole and Linda were unable to handle money. They were always asking us other siblings for money, and Linda became very pesky, always wanting to come visit or asking for money. It got to the point where none of us wanted anything to do with her. They lost their house and filed bankruptcy. They divorced after many years of marriage and many attempts by Cole to keep the family together.

Linda remarried, coincidentally to another man named Cole. They had the same kinds of problems as with the first marriage. Money was always a problem. They moved a lot and changed jobs often. I think Cole was good to Linda, but they too divorced and then remarried. Throughout Linda's tumultuous life, she somehow raised two nice young men. One of the sons now lives in Chicago and works in computers, and the other works the rodeo circuit out west. I recall that whenever I would see Linda's family, the boys were always neat, clean, and well behaved.

Despite all of Linda's problems, it was she that kept in touch with our mother. She apparently moved her from nursing home to nursing home after mom was released from the state hospital during the Reagan years. It is ironic that Linda couldn't really take care of herself, but that she watched out for our mom's care for all those years. Linda died of natural causes at the age of fifty. My wife; my sister, Michelle; and I attended the funeral. Very few people came to pay their respects. Afterward, I experienced some guilt because I felt that I could have been a better brother. Maybe if she had been allowed to remain at the home through high school, we would have been closer. I don't know. I felt bad that Linda had such a tough life. I never felt that her problems were caused by herself. She just never quite had the emotional capacity to deal with life's problems. I hope she is in heaven and is allowed some peace and tranquility.

Michelle was the middle child. She was almost two years older than me. Michelle was everyone's favorite. She was a very pretty girl, had a good personality, and won people over easily. Michelle and I were at the home the longest and have kept in touch all of our lives. We went through junior high and high school together and shared a lot of the same friends and acquaintances. We both lived in Burnside for many years after high school. Michelle still lives in Burnside. She has lived in the same house for thirty-five years and worked at the same job for thirty years.

Although Michelle and Colleen had a special sister relationship, Michelle and I were always pretty close. We were close enough in age that we usually attended the same schools and lived in the same buildings at the home. During junior high, we usually walked to and from school together. Throughout our life at the home, Michelle kept an eye on me. She sometimes had to counsel me or get after me for something I had done wrong or was doing that I shouldn't be. She was always a good big sister.

While in her fourth grade, Michelle fell in love with one of the boys from the home. His name was Jeremy. They became inseparable, which was a problem at the home. They dated all through high school, got married, and had two wonderful children. Unfortunately, they divorced after twenty-three years of marriage. They have since become good friends again, even though Jeremy remarried, and Michelle has been in a good relationship with another man for many years. Michelle and Jeremy's courtship for all those years at the home was difficult, but they really seemed to love each other. Michelle was very attractive and had lots of chances to date other boys, but she loved Jeremy. He was absolutely devoted to her. When they married, I was in the wedding. They used to invite me to their house for dinner often. I enjoyed their children, Scott and Gayla. One of Michelle's bosses used to say that she named her children after paper towels, Scott and Gala.

Jeremy was a very hard worker. He always had part-time jobs while in school, just like me. As an adult, Jeremy worked full-time in a factory and then moved to Eagle Foods, all the time still doing odd jobs to earn extra money to support his family. Michelle worked for the county for several years and then moved on to working for the U.S. government in one of the agricultural agencies. She has worked there for about thirty years and has since retired. Over the years, Michelle and Jeremy bought one house and then built their second home in unincorporated Burnside. Scott and Gayla are now in their thirties and have children of their own. Jeremy and Michelle worked very hard as parents to provide for their family and to keep the family together as a unit. I give them very high marks in that regard. They sure had no role models to emulate. They attended church regularly as a young family, and I think the association with people from the church was helpful to them. Like she was as a mom, Michelle has become a very dedicated and doting grandmother. Her family has always come first. I am sure she, like probably ever other child who went through the home, wants to make sure that like our own mother said, "You kids will never be in a home, like some other kids."

It was always the policy of the home and most court jurisdictions to attempt to keep all the children from broken families together, rather than have the children dispersed to various institutions and foster homes. Our situation was no different. Originally, Karen; the oldest; Linda, the youngest; and myself were brought to the home at one time on November 11, 1956. Michelle went to live with my Aunt Amelia, my mom's only sibling, in Auburn, Illinois and Colleen went to the same foster home in Auburn that I had just left. Both sisters came two or three years later. I recall that Michelle arrived at the home the same day we had gone to Brookfield Zoo. I always teased her, saying we had found her at the zoo.

The five of us were united for a few years. Linda had some pretty severe emotional problems and was not learning or adjusting well at school. In the fifth grade, she was taken to a foster home in Auburn. In Colleen's sophomore year, she was sent to live in Michigan.

I don't understand why they didn't just leave all five of us together. The funny part is that I was the one who wanted so badly to go to a foster home or be adopted. I think there is power in sibling emotional support. The home did a great job of caring for kids and the longer kids were at the home, the better adjusted they became. As we see much too often on the news today, the decision to pull kids away from their real home or send them to foster homes or institutions is a serious and difficult task. From my own personal observations, it seems that keeping the children together should be a first priority.

ACTIVITIES

In my freshman year, the home began taking us for a week-long visit to a camp near Madison, Wisconsin called Lake Waubesa Bible Camp. It was a very rustic setting on Lake Waubesa. There were cabins, a snack shop, dining hall, ball field, swimming pier, and a great raft out in the lake. It was a really nice way for all the kids to get a week at camp, even if our regular houseparents were there. There was camp staff there as well. It was fun being able to swim whenever we wanted and to see the girls in their bathing suits all the time. We enjoyed playing a lot of volleyball and baseball and wore ourselves out in the open air. Naturally, we had vespers each evening, which was a fancy name for a church service. Even vespers was more enjoyable with the chapel doors open and a fire going outside. Afterward, we would roast marshmallows and swim some more. Lake Waubesa was always an enjoyable trip to look forward to.

In the summer, we went to Lake Geneva Wisconsin, to Big Foot Beach, located just twenty miles north of Burnside, on a weekly basis. This was always a good time. The water was fun, the fresh air felt good, and we high school kids used this as an opportunity to pair off with the opposite sex. Once in a while, we were able to sneak across the street to the park area and have a cigarette or meet other kids who were not from the home. I remember one time we had gone off into the wooded area and came upon a young couple having sex. That was exciting for us to watch and to tell the other kids about.

The *Sound of Music* came out during the 1960s. It was one of the few movies that the home could fully endorse. They loaded all of us kids into the bus and drove us to the theater in Hinsdale, Illinois to see the film. Wow, that was the biggest theater I had ever been in. It was nothing like the local in Burnside. The only really nice thing about the local theater was that it had a balcony where you could make out pretty much uninterrupted. We spent quite a few evenings at the local show as it was one of the few activities we were allowed.

The home had a baseball field, football field and a couple of basketball hoops which we utilized. There was a TV that worked most of the time, a bowling machine someone had donated that was fun to play, but that was about it for things to do. Boredom always caused behavior problems. The old saying, "The idle mind is the devil's playground" is a truism. When we were bored, we would sit around and complain and feel sorry for ourselves. We would think of mischievous things to do. That's when kids would conspire to run away or think of ways to harass the houseparents. Boys and girls would pair off and make out or experiment sexually. Sometimes when school was out and there were no scheduled activities, all the kids would be home, but you would see no one. Somehow we all disappeared into our own little worlds or hiding places. Those were the kinds of days I did not like. I liked to be active and with other people, although I guess I had my own brooding times like everyone else.

A few years ago, I received my personal file from the home. For some reason, I had not completely read it until lately. I have shared most of it with my wife. She agrees with a lot of the assessments in the file that were made by house parents, and I can't argue with many of them. However, I think they may have been a little tough on me during my teen years. I had resentments like every kid who was there. I would have preferred being in an Ozzie and Harriet family environment, but I was not. I would have even accepted being in a nice foster home. Several references in the file by caseworkers indicated that placing me in foster care might have been a good idea, but it never happened for some reason or another. The caseworkers chided me for being involved in too many activities at church and school. Well, maybe I was trying to find happiness in my life or attempting to discover something in life besides church. I was only a teenager for crying out loud.

The people at the home liked me to be mature and follow the rules, but they didn't want me or anyone else asking too many questions or defying authority. This was the '60s and, believe me, kids were certainly questioning authority and defying their parents all across the country and around the world. We had a dorm council, of which I was elected president, so I sometimes posed questions that were brought up by the other kids. If the answers were not easy for the staff to answer, then we were being difficult. The home, the church, and the high school were bastions of rules, regulations, and hierarchy. That was a lot of pressure for me and the other kids to contend with. Everywhere we went, we were expected to behave in a certain way and follow a new set of regulations. We had very little freedom of choice about anything in our lives. If the caseworkers wrote some unkind things in my file, I can't imagine what they most have written about Misty Thompson, who pulled a knife on a houseparent. What must they have said about the kids who cussed and swore openly at their houseparents? How about the kids who ran away? What about the girls who were caught stealing clothes at Montgomery Wards on their way home from school? I guess I would like to see some of those files, but know that I never will. Still, I feel the caseworkers were a little hard on me.

I didn't realize it growing up, but the home had a lot of correspondence with the Kane County Court, as they were the official guardians of my family. Permission had to be granted for dental visits, vacations, spending for school clothes, and nearly everything else. I can see the reasons for this. Most of the requests in the file were in writing and were reasonable, as were the responses from the court. One response from the court stated that Kane County had spent over $33,000 in support of the Anderson children over the years. Today, that doesn't seem like such a big number, but in 1966, I guess it was. Over the years, I have spent a lot of time doing fundraising and volunteer work for many organizations. I think the reason for this is that I have wanted to pay back for the money that was spent supporting me and my sisters over the years. I hope I have done my part.

WEATHER

As I am sitting at my computer writing this story, it is raining very hard outside. It brings back memories of how the weather affected our lives as children at the home. Some of the kids were very scared of thunderstorms. When it rained hard, we always had water in the basement of the main building, which would cause the whole building to smell like mildew. Once in a while, we would have power outages, which would just be another reason for us to cause havoc. We always looked forward to snow days as a way of getting out of school—nothing different than today. A good snowfall probably was one of the best things to happen. It would make kids go outside and build snowmen, forts in the snow, and do snow angels. Sometimes we would sit near the highway and pummel cars with snowballs. We built some pretty awesome forts in the snow as I remember. When I got in high school and we would have a snow day, I would call one of my friends from school, and we would spend the day shoveling people's driveways. We earned some pretty good cash doing that. On days that the temperature was below zero, the home would take us to school in the bus. It was a little embarrassing being dropped off en masse like that, but the walk to either junior high or high school was over a mile and that made for a cold walk. We never had air conditioning at the home, so summers could be a little unbearable at times. The dorms had lots of windows which helped at night, but it was pretty tough to stay cool during the hot days of July and August. I do recall that there were window air conditioners in the office area where the executive director, business manager, and caseworkers sat though. The main building had at least two fireplaces, and the Heston House had two. They weren't used that often, but when they were, it was peaceful and helped to warm up the buildings.

THE GARDEN

Man, it's hot out here, and the mosquitoes just won't leave us alone. Why do we have to do this anyway? While I was living at the main building and in elementary school, the home had a huge garden. It must have been a half acre in size. We were required to spend time working in it as part of our chores. It was one of the chores that I really did not like to do. Even as an adult, I have never enjoyed a garden. We grew potatoes, tomatoes, sweet corn, beans, and I don't recall what all else. I don't know if the garden was just the fancy of the executive director at the time or what, but all of a sudden, they didn't have it anymore after I entered junior high. That was okay with me. I do have one good memory about the garden. One evening after dinner, we boys were sent out to weed as punishment for something we had done. Someone started throwing tomatoes. We really enjoyed ourselves for a while. By the time we were wore ourselves out slinging tomatoes, I think we had pretty much used up the whole crop for the season. We were a mess. We were all covered in red and looked like we had just been through a skirmish in Vietnam. Naturally, when the houseparent came out to check on us, he was astonished and angry. As punishment, we were required to put extra time in the garden for an entire week and, after showering, were sent right to bed for the night.

PHYSICAL LAYOUT OF THE HOME

There was a staff house located between the main building and the teen's residence. It was down a sidewalk that angled between the two buildings. Along the walk, peonies were planted and when in bloom were really beautiful. When I came to the home, the executive director, Mr. Taylor, and his family lived there. Soon thereafter, they bought a house and moved to the other side of town. A couple of different young couples with children lived there for a couple of years, and then it became home to several single women who worked at the home. I recall finding the house very beautiful. I am sure it was a pretty typical style for the time, but I wasn't used to carpeting throughout a home. The house had a small kitchen, an office—I had never seen on office in a home—a nice family room with a television and four bedrooms upstairs. Even the stairway had nice soft carpeting. There was a small screened in porch too. As a kid, I always thought I would like to live in that house as an adult. There was always a lot of traffic on that sidewalk that connected the two properties, with kids and houseparents going between buildings. One dark night, my oldest sister, Karen, had to go from one building to the other. Karen was always scared of the dark and was singing "Rock of Ages." I guess thinking that would protect her from the devil or the bogeyman. She made it all the way to the Henson House when my sister Colleen and another girl, Jolynn, jumped out from behind a bush and nearly gave Karen a heart attack. Karen never forgave Colleen for that.

When I first arrived at the home, the swing sets were located in the front yard of the property of the main building. The front yard was set back from the road and the swing set was probably 50' from a major state highway, which ran right in front of the home. I used to swing for long periods. We would push each other, and sometimes would even make ourselves go over the bars. That was scary, but fun. There was a teeter-totter specially attached at the other end. We always liked to get a new kid on one end, and when he was in the air and not paying attention, we would jump off the other end. That would make for quite a bounce on the butt for the new kid. It was just another rite of passage for the new kids to go through. I enjoyed watching the cars and got so I could identify nearly any car not only by its brand name but also the year of the car. This wasn't as difficult as it sounds because there weren't near as many makes or styles of cars as there are today. There was also a tether ball set there and a small merry go round type thing that could be spun around in circles. The harder it was pushed, the faster it would go and made it more difficult to hang on. One could be just standing still on it, and someone would always come by and give you a push. Visitors especially seemed to get a kick out of that, thinking they had just really made some kid's day. Eventually, the swing set was moved to a better location down near the ball field, where there was a set of monkey bars. This made more sense than being so close to the highway. I suppose it was because of budget constraints, but I never understood why the home didn't employ an athletic or activities director. We had a lot of land, some good facilities, and fifty children with lots of energy. I think it would have been good to keep us more active and occupied.

    The main building of the home was very large and very old. I found the building to be attractive. It had kind of a warm feel. It did not have a fence around it like some homes I have seen. There were nicely kept grounds and the building was always maintained well. We were good neighbors. When you entered the building, there was a small porch with three cement steps with railings. You had to go through the porch to ring the old-fashioned doorbell that had to be twirled in your fingers. Upon entering through that door, you could go to the right, which was the living room. This was the only room in the entire building that had carpet. It also had a fireplace and television. You were only allowed in the living room on special occasions or if you had visitors. Off of the living room was a small library that held books and games that we could access. It was never used as much as it should have been. On the other side of the front entrance was the office area where the administrative staff was housed. There were several offices where the executive director, the business manager, and the caseworkers worked; and there was an open area for several secretaries. There was also a washroom. If you came in the front entrance and went straight ahead, you would walk into the dining room. This was a large area, as it would seat about sixty people. There were tables of six and eight and then a big round dining table where staff and dignitaries would eat. In one corner was a milk machine and next to that was the dishwashing room.

On the other side of the dining room was the kitchen. The door to the kitchen was one of those doors that was cut in half so the bottom could be closed and the top left open for serving purposes. The kitchen was very institutional, with all metal sinks and counter areas. There was a huge old stove and a large refrigerator that looked more like a closet than a fridge. There was a small pantry just off the kitchen and a door leading down to the basement. We used to have to go down there to get canned goods or peel potatoes. I hated that. There were always rats in the basement. I would flash the lights and make all the noise I could before going down there, so I could scare the rats away. My future brother-in-law, Jeremy, liked to see the rats. He would open the door quickly, flip on the light, and make one big leap to the basement floor hoping to see the rats. Weird.

Off the kitchen was the back porch, the ironing room and a huge walk-in freezer.

To the left of the back porch was the recreation room as it was called. It was large and open. It had knotty pine walls and linoleum on the floor. We constantly had to mop and wax that floor, much to our chagrin. That room had a television, a bookcase that held a few books and games, a couple of small tables, a couch, and some odd chairs. That room probably got the most use of any room in the entire home, especially when the weather was inclement. At one time, the home used to show movies in the recreation room occasionally. There was an old-fashioned movie projector with the big round wheels. I don't know if it belonged to the home or to a houseparent, but it wasn't used long. We enjoyed those movie nights.

The second floor of the main building house the dorms for the children from first through eighth grade. There were two boys' dormitories. They were large wide open rooms that had ten to twelve beds in each dorm. Both dormitories had a bathroom, one with a tub. There was built-in storage area in both and one had some closet space. There was absolutely no privacy at any time in either dorm. You were even in public when you went to the bathroom. When anyone was upset or in trouble, everyone knew about it. If someone got a cold, everyone got a cold. Living that way was really troublesome for some boys. You could tell they really hated the life. I was luckier than most and was able to adjust. I just learned early on that you couldn't try to buck the system. You had to play along to survive.

The girls' dorm was nicer. That dorm was made up of rooms that held two to four beds. They had dressers in them. The girls had a little more privacy than the boys. That end of the building had a larger bathroom with more amenities. Even the stairway going up to the girls' dorm was better.

It was wider and had carpeting on the stairs. At the end of the floor by the girls' dorm was the houseparent's apartment, which consisted of a bedroom, living room, and kitchen. It was small but private. At the other end of the building, between the two boys' dormitories, was a small room with a toilet, where a houseparent slept sometimes. I occupied that room during my senior year in high school, as I served as kind of a night proctor for the boys. It was nice having my own room, and it allowed me some additional freedoms.

The basement of the main building was huge. It housed the shower area for the boys and a large room that held lockers for each boy. The rest of the room was filled with whatever junk or possessions any of us owned or brought home with us. The rest of the basement was used for storage of food stuffs and canned goods. The basement was always damp and cold, a little bit scary, especially because of the rats. There was a ping-pong table which we used a lot. One boy had a nice train set down there at one time which all of us admired and observed.

Other buildings on the property with the main building were a small cottage for house parents located just a few feet away from the main building. This cottage had a small basement where the boiler for the main building was located. The cottage had a small kitchen, bathroom, living room, and one bedroom. It housed a lot of different house parents over the years. Attached to the cottage was a very tall brick chimney.

About thirty feet east of the cottage was the laundry housed. The ground floor was where all clothing donations would come to the home. The room was always filled with clothing of all sizes, shapes, and vintages. There were built-in wooden bins that all the dirty laundry was sorted into. The basement contained the huge washing machine, extractor for taking water out of the clothes, and the gigantic dryer. I, like most of the older boys, had a stint at doing laundry as a part-time job. It wasn't a bad chore, except when you had to do sheets for manor. So much of the bedding was soiled by the old people who had become incontinent. That was pretty smelly. It was exciting at first to operate the laundry equipment, but even that became a chore after a while. At the other end of the basement of the laundry house was the cellar. This is where potatoes and some vegetables were stored. I hated going in there. It was damp, stunk like mildew, had spiders and sometimes mice.

Just east of the laundry house was a small tool shed where the lawn-mowing equipment, rakes, shovels, and various tools were stored. That facility was always locked. The lawn was mowed by the maintenance man. There must have been some kind of insurance liability issue with having kids operate the mower, or they would have had us doing that chore.

Next in line was the chicken coop, where I lost my virginity at the age of twelve. This was just a vacant chicken coop that was occupied by junk and seldom used items. I remember we used to use the structure for cleaning fish after being taken fishing. The maintenance man would sometimes use the building for spanking kids. We got caught smoking in there one time by him. He made us smoke corn stalks until we puked. He thought that would cure us of the desire to smoke. It did not, but it was a good try. At some point, someone installed a basketball hoop on side of the chicken coop. We got a lot of good use out of that.

Until one of the boys burned it down, Annie Kugler's old spooky Bates Motel of a house occupied the next lot. That house was separated from the chicken coop and garden by a gravel road that gave rear access between the main building and the Henson House. Annie's house should have been destroyed long before it was. I suppose the home had dreams of someday putting it to some use, but the house was just too old and decrepit. Then again, it was good for telling scary stories.

The Henson House, for the teens, was located in the next block going south on the highway. It was separated from the main building property by a small residential street with only one other house on it.
The Henson House had been a part of the Dodd School for Boys at one time and the Home bought the property in the 1950s to house the teenage boys and girls. It was a two-story, brick structure with a porch on one side. Actually, the porch was originally the front of the building, but a new entrance was put on the side facing the highway. The porch had a nice wooden swing that was used by everyone. There was a canopy drive through at one end of the building, but no garage. There was a gravel parking lot for several cars and a circular drive. The building sat back about seventy feet from the highway. The building has since been destroyed and is part of the day care center that the home eventually evolved into.
There were a lot of stairs in that building. Upon entering the front door, you could choose between two small flights of stairs, one of which went to the basement or you could go straight ahead into the main part of the building. Going straight, there was a small chapel to the right. The chapel was very nice. There was an altar, burgundy carpeting, and four small pews with padding to match the carpet. The chapel was for children or adults to use as desired for praying, devotions, or a private visit.

There was a fairly large room across the hall that was used for many different purposes over the years. Sometimes it was used as a staff person's room and sometimes as kind of a craft area. Going straight ahead, there was a hallway that had a closet and storage area and to the left was the sick room, where a child would be placed if he or she needed to be kept away from other children while suffering from measles or something like that.

Then there was the large common area on the first floor. This is where everyone congregated and mingled before heading to their respective rooms or going out somewhere. This was convenient as it was next to the office where the houseparent would sit and keep track of our comings and goings. A file cabinet was kept in the office that held folders and records of each of us. The office was used for private consultations with kids too. On the other side of the communal room was the houseparent's apartment. There were French doors that could be closed when they wanted privacy. Their quarters were nice. The living room was carpeted and had a fireplace. There was nice-size kitchen, a bedroom, and a private bath for them. Depending upon the individual houseparent and whether or not they had children of their own, the family room was sometimes used by the kids for visitation purposes.

From a different direction of the communal room, you would take another stairway up to the girl's dorm. It wasn't really a dorm. There were five bedrooms, each with two beds, and there was a nice bathroom for the girls to share. On the other side of the house, the boy's dorm had four bedrooms. Three of the rooms had two beds and one only had room for one bed, and occasionally had a bunk bed in it. During my stay at Harrison House, I occupied all of the rooms at one time but liked it best when I was able to stay in the room by myself with the one bed. It was small but private. I was very particular about neatness and cleanliness and being by myself made that easier to accomplish. There was a bathroom on the floor that had a stool, urinal, two sinks, and a shower.

At one end of the boy's dorm was another stairway that led up to the attic. That was kind of a cool attic. It was finished off with drywall and a hardwood floor. There wasn't much stored up there, except an old stuffed turtle that scared all new kids when they first saw it. We used to sneak up to the attic at night and lay by the window and smoke cigarettes.

There was a roof over the porch that spanned between the dorms, and boys and girls would sometimes use the roof as a path to each other's rooms. Someone got caught at some point, and then bars were put over the windows. Darn! There was a metal fire escape along one side of the building that was by the girls' dorm. Girls used it to sneak out at night. At some point, an alarm of some type was put on the window that went out to the fire escape.

The stairway from the girls' dorm went all the way down to the basement. The basement was finished very nicely. There was a large room that was paneled and had a tile floor that housed a television area, a bowling machine that someone had donated, a ping-pong table, pool was not allowed, and a couch and chairs. There was a fireplace on one end of the basement. Along one wall was a room with a wrestling mat in it. Boys would wrestle in there and sometimes box. We had a couple of houseparents that made boys "put on the gloves" when they got into fights. There was a hallway that ran along the television area that led to the boiler room and then the laundry area. The laundry area had an iron and ironing board, a washer, and dryer. There were shelves for hangers, soap, bleach, etc. When girls reached high school, laundry became their own responsibility. The boys were charged with outside maintenance of the building but still got their laundry taken care of.

The Heston House was really a nice facility for the teenagers. It allowed some form of privacy, and kids could feel closer to someone as a roommate than they could residing in a large dorm.

There was usually a place in the building or on the property where you could have a friend over for a visit. It is ironic that we were always trying to get away from the home and loved to go to other people's homes to visit, but there were a lot of kids from school that enjoyed coming to the home to visit. Some of these kids just liked the individuals they were visiting and some liked having a lot of kids around. As I grew older and met some of the parents of these young people, I understood better why they liked to visit the home. Their home lives were not good, and they realized that we were at least in a safe and caring environment. We didn't always get along with each set of houseparents, but none of us ever felt threatened by physical abuse or violence. We knew we would have three meals a day and a warm bed to sleep in. Some of the kids from school did not have that assurance.

The building was done very well, was structurally very sound, and was always well maintained. The grounds were attractive. The front had a nice grassy area, divided by a sidewalk, and there were mature trees on the property. I actually felt the building was a little like a frat house. "Animal House" may have been a more appropriate name than Heston House, given the way we acted and the shenanigans we pulled. There were some heartbreaking times during the five years I spent at Heston House, but there were some fun times too.

To the east of the Heston House was the old Dodd School football field. There were no longer any yard lines, goal posts or bleachers, but there were still some remains of the cinder track. We used it to play baseball and touch football. Next to the field was the infamous "Dodd barn." This had originally been used for horses, but no horses had been on the property for years. We used the building as a place to be alone, hide, smoke, and have sex. With the hayloft on the second floor and a window there, it made for a good spot for a lookout in case houseparents headed that way, which they rarely did for some reason. There was a basketball hoop and a very nice wooden backboard installed on the barn.

Bordering the property by the barn was Vineyard Street. The home owned three houses on that street that different house parents lived in over the years. During my late teens and very early twenties, I lived in all three of those houses at different times. Two were small ranch-style homes and one was a large, old two-story. All the houses had detached garages, which were very typical of houses built at that time. The home did a good job of maintaining their properties, both from a functional and an aesthetic standpoint.

The Masons had bought one of the buildings from Dodd School and converted it into a Masonic Lodge. It was just south of the Henson House. They would allow the home to use the building for parties occasionally. They also put on parties for us once in a while. I met a lot of the men who were in the Masonic Lodge and remained friends with some of them and their children for many years.

Next to the Masonic Lodge was the abandoned Dodd School gymnasium. The building needed to be torn down, but it still had a decent basketball court on the second floor that we used sometimes. The lower level was just old shower rooms and lockers. It was kind of a scary old building, but we got some good use out of it.

From the gym to the end of the block, which was the intersection of two major highways, sat the Burnside Residence. That had been the residential portion of Dodd School for Boys, and someone had purchased the building and turned it into an old people's home. There was an old abandoned swimming pool on the property. We used to use the glass cover for target practice with rocks and sling shots. The residence looked good from the outside with a nicely kept lawn and signage area, but inside it was disgusting. The odor of urine was terrible. The residence, as we referred to it, was on my paper route, and I had to go in their five days a week. Not only did it stink, but I was turned off by the sight of the old and decrepit people sitting around bored to death. A few of the high school girls worked at the residence once in a while. They had awful stories to tell about the condition of the place and the way old people were treated. Naturally, at my young age, the people seemed even older than they were. When I was in high school, I used to be invited to the residence to sing at programs put on by the staff. I don't mean to be unfair in describing the residence. The manor that was operated by Burnside Homes was only a quarter mile up the highway, and I was in that facility very often because of the relationship with the children's home. The Manor was definitely cleaner, better kept, and the residents seemed much happier and better cared for.

PETS

I have been a dog lover my entire adult life. Pets were not really allowed at the home. Mr. Taylor's family had a boxer that was always around the home because the Taylors lived on the property at the time, and there were occasional stray dogs or cats that would show up, but dogs and cats were not allowed. Once in a while, some kid would bring home a bird or hamster that someone gave them. Most houseparents tried to be reasonable and understanding about these things, but they never worked out. There were just too many kids with too many desires and differing agendas to have pets or small animals around the buildings. It caused unnecessary problems for kids and staff as well.

One time, I bought a ticket for a fund-raiser for the AFS chapter at school, and I won a goose. It came in a cage, and I kept it outside on the back lawn of the Henson House. I didn't care for it. It was noisy, dirty, and unfriendly. I finally traded it to a houseparent for a pair of shoes. He sold some sort of shoes on the side. I don't know what he did with the goose. It was gone from the property in a few days. Maybe he cooked it. I can't remember the house parent's name, but he was an odd duck himself.

JOBS

I worked a lot of different jobs while growing up at the home and other kids did as well. My sister, Michelle, worked at the local dairy queen for a couple of years. Shonda worked part-time in a beauty salon and went on to get her license as a beautician. Jordan worked for a local car dealer. Some of the teens found jobs working in retail stores. Most of the teenage girls had regular babysitting jobs. I think it spoke well for the home that the girls there were considered a good source for babysitters. Some of the girls had jobs cleaning people's homes. Some of the boys did lawn mowing for people on a regular basis. In the summer, the kids would sometimes find work in groups, such as detasseling corn or working on a vegetable farm. I remember one man who used to come with two vehicles and pick up a bunch of kids to work on his vegetable farm for weeks at a time. I guess we were like day laborers. We were always looking out for each other on the employment front. We all needed money, and we all wanted a chance to be away from the daily drudgery of home life. Several of the kids were just like me. They became attached to their employers, especially if it was more of a one-on-one situation. When this happened, the kid would usually end up spending a lot of time with the employer/friend. I think most of these relationships were healthy and good for the young people, but the relationships were resented by other kids because it generally meant we got a few more privileges. I think the houseparents liked the relationships, and sometimes turned a blind eye to the situation because they knew we were in good hands, not getting in trouble and it was just that many more kids the house parent didn't have to worry about each day.

One very unusual incident happened with one of the girls babysitting. Mindy Jones was babysitting at a house on the corner of Woodridge and Airport Streets one night. A fire broke out, and she was credited with saving the baby's life. It created quite a media stir locally for a while.

THE BIG HOUSE

Sometimes prisons are referred to as the Big House. I don't want anyone to think that I considered life at the Burnside Children's Home to be a prison, although I know that some kids thought felt like they lived in a prison. There were definite similarities in the daily routines, regimentation, and how adults dealt with the children. When I watch movies or television shows about prison life, it always reminds me of the home. With humor, I will attempt to make an analogy.

As teenagers, we lived in small rooms (cells) with one other person. We shared secrets and hid things from the other kids and houseparents. We found ways to deceive the adults and to connive with one another to protect ourselves. A favorite punishment was to send us to our cells. If a child was sent to his or her room for an extended period of time, we said they were put in solitary confinement. There were bed checks of our cells by the houseparents (guards). If there was a problem such as someone missing, we would all be woken up and called to order (roll call). Sometimes we were put in a lockdown mode, with every kid being sent to their cell for quiet time or as a form of controlling the general population."

There was an executive director (warden) of the home that all of us kids feared. None of us wanted to be sent to his office for reprimanding or counseling. That would not turn out well—we knew. The warden had the final say and all the power at the home. If he gave an order, it had to be followed.

We ate in a dining room (mess hall), much like in prisons. The big difference was that we served family style instead of having to go through a line. Once we were seated, it was much like prison life. Bigger or tougher kids taking food from smaller kids, kids being kicked under the table for saying the wrong thing, food being withheld by a houseparent because of some infraction were just some of the similarities at feeding time. The plates and silverware were very utilitarian in design. The tables and chairs were institutional in nature.

At the main building, when I was younger, everything was done by the bell. A bell was rung when it was time to get up and another bell was rung at fifteen minutes before each meal, giving us time to wash our hands and get into line before entering the mess hall.

In the summertime a bell was rung in the evening to let us know it was time for all kids to come in for the night. Then we were all gathered in the recreation room and required to be quiet and settle down for the night. At one half hour before lights out, we were sent to our dorms. We had thirty minutes to bathe, go to the bathroom, and everyone get quiet. We had devotions and then lights out.

The home (prison) had all of the familiar sounding names for different parts of the institution. We had a chapel, and the local preacher was our chaplain. There was an infirmary where we were sent for minor scrapes, bruises, and medication. We even had a room that was used as sick bay. There was the yard outside where we were allowed to exercise and congregate.

When new kids came, they were always given a tour, and the rules were explained to them. They were told who was boss, what was expected of them, and what the consequences would be if rules were not followed.

Depending upon the houseparents, we sometimes felt like inmates. Some of the house parents were warmer and friendlier, but some just thought of us as inmates or cattle, just going through the motions with us and providing three meals a day and a warm place to sleep. I'm sure all of these measures were necessary, and the home certainly did not operate like a prison, but the analogy comes pretty naturally.

PREPARING US FOR ADULT LIFE

The home did what they could to teach us about preparing ourselves for adult life. One of the ways was to teach us about saving money. I believe it was when Rev. Keating came to the home that this practice started. Rev. Keating had a reputation for being a great money manager, and he wanted to help us learn.

We had to turn in any money we got from any source—jobs, allowances, money received as gifts—to the current houseparent. The money would be allocated into a two different accounts. One account was a forced savings account, which was the money that was not to be touched by us until it had served its purpose. The purpose had to be for a large item, such as a car when we left the home or money to be used for college. The other account was a simple savings account that we could access with permission from our houseparent. The home put the money in the bank, and we were paid interest on our money. The only problem with this system was that it taught, forced, us kids to save money, but I don't think it taught us how to spend money responsibly. As a result, many of the kids who left the home had financial problems as adults. When they got their hands on money and no one was controlling it, they simply spent it like a drunken sailor. I know that several of the kids went on as adults to file bankruptcy, only adding to their other problems.

The home certainly taught us about cleanliness and order. They taught us the importance of doing daily chores and duties. Any child who spent much time at the home knew about hard work. The girls were taught how to cook, do laundry, and iron. The boys, however, did not really receive any kind of training. I regret that I never learned anything about plumbing or electricity. I think the home would have been better off encouraging the aid of an industrial arts instructor or some local artisans to help teach the boys at the home some basics about home ownership or auto repair rather than all the time they spent teaching us about music and studying the Bible. As was the case so often, priorities were established by whoever was in charge at the time. Since the home was run by the church, priorities were church related. I guess the other reason that there was no real plan for the boys was that a lot of kids were not at the home for that long of a time, and any class would have been disrupted by the constantly changing population.

The home certainly tried to teach each of us to have a relationship with God. Each of the kids had their own ideas in this regard. Some kids grew up to lead solid Christian lives. Other kids totally rejected the church and religion, but I would guess that most children who went through the home, especially if they were there for any length of time, knows the value of a spiritual life and has some sort of religious aspect to their life. Religion aside, we certainly were taught the difference between right and wrong. Everything at the home was pretty much black and white, not many shades of grey. All of my adult life, I have always tried to do what is right. It has always been a pretty easy decision for me, as I had an instinctive feel for what was the right thing to do. That had been driven into me for twelve years.

If we wanted to learn to drive, we had to do that on our own. Of course we had to take Driver's Ed at school, but to go on and get a permit and then a license, we had to find an adult with a car who would let us practice driving and then accompany us to take the test. Because it was the policy of the home to not allow kids to own cars, it was easy to discourage us from even getting licenses. A lot of the kids did get their licenses and drove any chance we got.

Houseparents always tried to make sure that we dressed nice. We were not allowed to go to school looking like we had nothing. Fortunately, we did not have to wear uniforms or any clothing that identified us as "kids from the home." The girls, especially, were monitored in their dress. Skirts had to be a certain length, and all clothing had to be modest. The girls, then as now, would sometimes take a separate set of clothes to school and change when they got there. Mainly, the boys had to have clean clothes. We were taught to shine our shoes, which I still do diligently to this day.

I recall at some point, maybe around the eighth grade, the home decided that all of the boys should get a new suit. Most of us to that point did not own a suit. We were taken to Robert Hall, a now out of business popularly priced men's clothing chain, and allowed to pick out a suit. I really liked that. My suit was a dark olive green in a nice hard finish. I wore it proudly and took good care of it.

THE CHURCH

Throughout my book I make many references to the church. That is the church that originally started the home over 120 years ago and operated it for about ninety years. *Free* was hardly the correct word to describe the church in the minds of us kids. We resented the rules established by the church that forbade us from attending dances and movies. We felt it was much too strict. The Church split with the traditional fundamentalist church back in the 1800s over the issue of slavery and also for the charging of people to sit in the pews of the church. While the church was more liberal for its time of origin, we felt like it kept us imprisoned.

The church provided a lot of support for the home through its network of churches in the country but mostly churches in the central Midwestern part of the country. I think every church in the region had a line item in their budget for the Burnside Homes, which referred to the Children's Home and the village, the old people's home. Every year at Thanksgiving time, the general church would hold what was called Harvest Fest. Members of the congregation would donate money, food, bedding, clothing, and pharmacy items to the home. This provided a lot of food and necessary items for us. Sometimes it was delivered by the truckload, and we were required to unload the truck and stack the food items in the basement or pantry. This was hard but necessary work on our part. Harvest Fest was one of those times when several of us kids were called upon to visit other churches, sometimes on just Sunday morning and sometimes Sunday morning and evening. There were even some special services on a Wednesday or Saturday evening we attended. We would "sing for our supper" as we called it. I sang solos. We also had a girl, Chenoa, that I sang duets with. There was a girl's trio at one time, and at another point, there was very small choral group. The singing groups always depended upon the make-up of the children at the time. The groups became a little more accomplished in high school because Reverend Keating's wife, a music major in college, began directing us. After services, we were generally treated to a meal in someone's home, which was always nice. We then had to load up the car or truck with that church's donations. The houseparent always picked up a check. While Harvest Home provided a great deal of support, it is another example of the hypocritical attitude the church and home had about Sunday activities. We could not play ball or engage in any kind of commerce on Sundays, but it was acceptable for us kids to be used to do fundraising for the home on a Sunday. That always made me a little angry, but I was willing to do my part. I felt I owed that much to the home and the church for all they had done for me.

I was active in nearly all church activities that I could take part in. I found it a good way to keep busy, make friends, and learn more about the world and adulthood. I made friends with kids my age and also some of their parents. When I look back, I realize that church was one of the places that I learned about **connecting** and **networking** with people. These activities have come naturally to me in my career as a banker.

One of the downsides of my being so involved with the church was that it made me stand out. Many people from the congregation thought it was their responsibility to keep an eye on me, as well as other kids from the home, and make our business their business. Supposedly, these people had our best interest at heart, but we felt they were spying on us and being nosy. If we did anything that was not in strict accordance with their beliefs, they were quick to call houseparents with the news. I remember one of the church elders calling the home and telling them that I had been walking toward the high school with my arm around a girl. People were always calling to say they had seen one of the kids smoking and had seen one of them riding in a car. There were some very nice people from the church as well. Some of them provided part-time work for us kids. We mowed loans, raked leaves, washed windows, and did whatever jobs we could find. The home was a constant source for babysitters. Once in a while, people from the church expected us to do work for free, but generally, we were paid. One job we always seemed to get was to help people move. The home owned several rental properties near the campus that were used to serve as homes for houseparents. Whenever people moved in or out, the teenage boys were expected to help with the moving. People from the church were always calling on us for that as well. To this day, I do not like to help people or myself move. Even though I became pretty proficient at the process, I guess I just had my fill of it during high school.

Most of the houseparents who worked at the home came there through some affiliation with the church. They attended one of the churches, had attended one of the church's colleges, or maybe had answered an ad in the ***Burnside Friend*** publication. Most of the houseparents did not stay for long periods. There were a few exceptions, but I don't think most stayed more than one year. Being a houseparent was a full-time commitment. The job was difficult, the pay was low, and I think there was a considerable amount of heartbreaking experiences. It seemed that most of them were in a transitional period in their lives. They were maybe finishing up their education, fulfilling some educational requirement, were between jobs that were ones they were really not interested in, or were just trying to find out what they really wanted to do with their lives. I do believe they were all loving, kind, and sincere people, whether being a houseparent was their calling or not.

We occasionally had people from the church who would be substitute houseparents for a day or evening when the home had difficulty with scheduling or an emergency might have arisen for the regular houseparents. This was a treat for us. It was like having a substitute teacher. They really didn't know the rules and were easy to take advantage of. Plus, I think they felt sorry for us and wanted to be nice. Most of these people who helped out at these times came back fairly regularly so I guess we didn't treat them too badly. These were the people from the church who seemed to have our genuine interest at heart. I don't know for sure, but I would guess that they were among the ones who so generously fulfilled our wish lists at Christmas time.

As if we didn't get enough religion on a daily basis at the home, someone introduced us to Youth For Christ or YFC. Youth for Christ is an international organization for teenagers, based out of Wheaton, Illinois. I drive by their offices often. It is a fundamentalist organization that helps bring teenagers to Christ. We met at the home, and I was elected the first president of our local chapter. There were a lot of good activities sponsored by the group that usually took place on Saturday evenings. We went roller skating, attended Christian music concerts, went on hayrides, and other wholesome activities. No dances though. There was always a religious context to the events. We all knew the purpose of the group so that was okay. On June 16, 1964, I was given a very handsome, red leather-bound YFC Bible. I know the exact date because I wrote it on the inside cover. It was a gift from Don and Joan Major. I don't recall the occasion, and it really doesn't coincide with any significant date. I still have the Bible and treasure it. I do not read it as often as I should. A few years ago, I received a letter from a gentleman from the church who helped with our YFC chapter. He sent me a business card that we had printed up that had me listed as president of the group. I have kept the memento. This man provides an interesting aside to my story. He was always very vocal in church about his Christianity, but I learned after I left the home that this man used to beat his wife and kids.

Reading my story, some people may get the impression that I resented the church. I do not. Some of the kids really hated the church and anyone that had anything to do with it. I think this had to do more with rejection of authority on any level and the fact that they simply did not like the structure of the church than really with religion itself. Some of the rules were difficult to contend with, but I knew they were necessary and also that the church had the right to make them since they provided so much support. Although I had a few not so pleasant experiences with the church, my general conclusion is that the church provided a very positive experience for me and has had a lasting effect on my life. I have strong beliefs that I learned from the church that have guided me throughout my life. People from the church were really my foundation for those many years I was at the home. I probably would not have survived without them. The church was a constant in my life, and I could always count on people there for help.

EPILOGUE

I am now sixty-five years old, just signed up for Medicare, and recently retired. That word *retired* doesn't sound right to me. I have worked so hard all my life. For at least half of my adult life, I have worked two jobs at once. I have owned several businesses, a men's clothing store, a costume jewelry store, a pest control business, and a residential cleaning business. I enjoyed over twenty years in commercial banking. I served eight years as a city councilman and four years as mayor of a small city. I have been involved with many charity and volunteer groups. I have been busy all my adult life. Now it is time to slow down. I can tell physically that I don't have the energy that I once had. Now is when I should spend more quality time with my wonderful wife, Deborah. I need to enjoy our boxer dogs that we rescue. It is also a time to reflect, I suppose.

Every time I work on this book, I get reminded of other people or stories about people who lived at or were associated with the Burnside Children's Home. I suppose I could write about it for a long time, but the line needs to be drawn somewhere.

Briefly, I will tell you that living in the home prepared me for my life and its myriad experiences. All of the experiences I have had were influenced by my upbringing there, just as most people's lives are influenced by the actions, directions, and guidance of their own parents.

The home taught me to care about others. I learned that volunteerism and doing good are basic life rules that we should all adhere to. Volunteering and helping others is good for the soul. I saw that by observing the many people who gave of their time, money, and efforts to see that the children raised in the home had relatively happy lives.

I learned that one has to work hard to succeed. I saw that one could simply survive in life by accepting help from the government, churches, and charities; but to really succeed, one needs to work. Not only work at a job, or two, but to work at life, to put forth the extra effort required to get through each day, and, hopefully, to prepare for the future.

I learned that one has to get along with others. You have to take care of yourself, but you also need to respect the rights and ideas of those around you.

Probably the most valuable lesson I have learned over the years is that no matter how bad things may seem or how hard things are at times, there are always people out there who have it worse. I have seen that there are very few perfect, if any, families. All families have their problems, secrets, and misfortunes. The home taught me to deal with adversity and disappointment. I learned that things do get better most of the time. It is better to confront the problems head on rather than ignore them or turn to drugs or alcohol for solace.

I sincerely hope that some people, after reading **The New Kid** will feel inspired or motivated to deal with problems in their lives, will work to rekindle family relationships, and will try to mentor or help young people who are going through tough times. I hope that readers will feel the need to become the kind of people I was fortunate enough to learn from at the Burnside Children's Home.

Edwards Brothers Malloy
Thorofare, NJ USA
January 14, 2015